CW01480934

CLEMO T]

Study and Colloquy

by

Brian Louis Pearce

Magwood

2002

CLEMO THE POET

Study and Colloquy

by

Brian Louis Pearce

ISBN 0 946603 14 6

Cover photo © Maurice Gabb, 2002:
Jack Clemo at Weymouth, 1977

Cover design by Neil Annat

Published by
Magwood
72 Heathfield South,
Twickenham,
Middlesex, TW2 7SS

Acknowledgements
Besides the references in the notes or text I should like to
acknowledge my indebtedness to *Coeli et Terra, Eternal
Anthology 3* (Raunchland), *Iota, The Journal, The Proper Fuss,
Reformed Quarterly, Stride, The Swansea Review, Third Way*;
Ruth (nee Peaty) and the late Jack Clemo, Bella Peaty, Michael
Spinks [for his constant help including the sketch-map of
Goonamarris*], Tricia and David Porter, Maurice Gabb, the late
Donald Davie; Daniel Jenkins, Clyde Binfield, Alan Gaunt,
Louis Hemmings, Graham Hedges, Rupert Loydell, David Miller,
Tony Bryer, Nia Taylor, Patricia Nicholls, Philippa Lausen,
Marian Wood, my wife Margaret and daughter Ann; the Dorset
County Museum (Dorchester), the Wheal Martyn Museum (nr.
St Austell), and Tricia Porter Photography for permission to use
the photographs of Ruth, Jack, his mother and the cottage, taken
at Goonamarris in 1975. In the summer of 2001 three of Tricia
Porter's photographs of Jack were accepted by the National
Portrait Gallery, London.

                              BLP/ Twickenham/ 2001

*Shortly to put us further in his debt with his forthcoming
biography of Clemo.

Contents

A Clemo Checklist

[poetry marked *]

Wilding Graft: novel	Chatto & Windus, 1948
	Anthony Mott, 1983
Confession of a Rebel:	Chatto & Windus, 1949, 1975
autobiography	Spire [Hodder & Stoughton], 1988
**The Clay Verge*	Chatto & Windus, 1951
*[‘The Wintry Priesthood’:	[Arts Council], Harmondsworth,
sequence in] *Poems 1951*	Middlesex, Penguin, 1951
The Invading Gospel	Bles. 1958
	London, Lakeland, 1972
	Basingstoke, Marshall Pickering, 1986
* *The Map of Clay*	Methuen, 1961
[including *The Clay Verge,* 'The Wintry Priesthood', 'Frontier Signals']	
*[Selection in]	Harmondsworth, Middlesex, Penguin,
Penguin Modern Poets 6	1964
**Cactus on Carmel*	Methuen, 1967
**The Echoing Tip*	Methuen, 1971
**Broad Autumn*	Methuen, 1975
The Marriage of a Rebel:	Gollancz, 1980
autobiography	Spire [Hodder & Stoughton], with extra chapter, 1988
**The Bouncing Hills*:	Redruth, Truran, [1983]
dialect tales and light verse	
**A Different Drummer*	Padstow, Tabb House, 1986
The Shadowed Bed: novel	Tring, Lion, 1986
**Selected Poems*	Newcastle upon Tyne, Bloodaxe Books, 1988

Banner Poems:
a decade of Cornish Verse

Gorran, St Austell,
CNP Publications, 1989

Clay Cuts [selection with
woodcuts by Stan Dobbin]

Church Hanborough, Oxford,
Previous Parrot Press, 1991

Approach to Murano

Newcastle upon Tyne,
Bloodaxe Books, 1993

The Cured Arno

Newcastle upon Tyne,
Bloodaxe Books, 1995

The Clay Kiln: novel

St Austell,
Cornish Hillside Publications,
2000

pre and post - 1968/70

Tavistock

Mineral Railway

To Exeter

To Callington

Trefren china clay Works

Gunnees china clay Works

Gunnees LG office

filter pressess & spouts

Treolaget settling pit

Treolago School (now head teacher's house)

Treolago Methodist church

Road layout pre - 1968/70

clerks' cottage

Gwennarnix

Clemo the Poet: a study

A Calvinist aesthete. A blind and deaf seer and mystic. A latter-day Bunyan, self-taught in essence, reared in a stone cottage amid the Cornish clay-pits, who became a widely read and published poet, and who communicated widely, over a long lifetime, with all sorts and conditions of men, literary and otherwise. A passionate man, not afraid to be honest about himself and the human condition, who sought love and marriage over many years and eventually found it and, with it, abundant happiness. A Methodist who didn't go to church for thirty years, then attended a Baptist chapel, and whose sympathies and subjects as a poet, Calvinist fundamentalist as he remained in essence, were as hospitable to Roman Catholic as to Salvation Army or (in his own words) 'hot-gospel' expression and inspiration.[1]

A thoroughly straightforward, kindly, homely man, who radiated goodwill and common sense, whose thought was deep and clear; whose subjects were uncommon for his time yet timeless, and ended his life with one of the best-stocked minds of his generation. A man who spent most of his life in Cornwall, followed by a decade in Weymouth, whose last collections reflect his experience of Italy, especially Florence and the Venetian Lagoon. His poetry is an unusual bond of sensuous and cerebral reaction to a place, a mood, a person (historical or contemporary), and of a theme with the imagery of its real or imagined setting. Some of his poetry is unstructured; some of it is loosely rhymed in arbitrary paragraphs - as it seems to me, though Donald Davie[2] rates one of these, 'Mould of Castile', as Clemo's 'finest poem' – and some of it, especially in his earlier (and mid) career, is structured and rhymed, shaped and worked liked the finest pottery, and constitutes, to my judgement, the first of two peaks, the second being the best of the dramatic monologues and other *person-responsive* poems to be found in *The Echoing Tip* and *Broad Autumn* period. His poetry widened in sympathy and subject range over the years, but the enduring artefacts hail, for the most part, from these two sources: the earlier 'clay-pit' (emotional and environmental) experiences, and the mellowing of his vision and broadening of his range associated with his marriage. His novels and other writings are of significance, not least as an aid to understanding his poetry. But it is his poetry *per se* which is the subject of this study.

The poet Clemo consists, then, of elements that could be thought of as being in conflict. Yet these diverse elements existed happily and constructively in one frame, and contributed to his fecund and original artistry. Let us see how this came about.

I *Reginald John Clemo* was born on March 11th, 1916, in a farmhouse near St Austell. His father, an illiterate clay-kiln worker, was killed in the First World War, and Jack was brought up by his Methodist mother in a small cottage at Goonamarris, remorselessly invaded over the years by the clay tips and pit workings. It was an austere landscape, and mindscape, too, for one born into a strict stratum of Calvinism[3] and who began to suffer attacks of blindness from the age of five, losing his hearing by the end of his teens, and his sight by the age of 39. There was the lack of understanding, too, perhaps inevitable, given the period, his erotic/mystical fulcrum, his literary interests, and his inability to play a normal working-man's part in that somewhat isolated, bleakly industrial setting. He was well on in years when the chapel folk said to Ruth Clemo (nee Peaty): 'Tell Jack to write something we can understand'.[4]

His grandfather had been a local preacher and there had been three Methodist ministers in the family. His cousin Joseph Hocking, the novelist, was a Methodist minister, a fellow Cornishman and miner's son. But 'Jack was regarded as a recluse standing bent and frail in his mother's cottage garden with his black beret and dark glasses, already going blind, already afflicted by deafness,' writes Ray Trudgian.[5]

These were the lonely, difficult years yet, far from giving way to his manifold frustrations, Jack used them to energise the growing unity in diversity of his literary, psychological, sexual and religious pilgrimage. His emphasis upon Christian gusto is in line with Daniel Jenkins' 'contrapposto' or harmony in discord[6-7], and unites his entire physical, mental and spiritual being in one creative energy.

Breakthrough came with the publication of his first novel *Wilding Graft* in 1948; publication of his first volume of autobiography *Confession of a Rebel* in 1949; the Chatto and Windus volume of poetry *The Clay Verge* (1951), and his prize winning sequence *The Wintry Priesthood*, one of eight poets' work published by Penguin as *Poems 1951*. These two groups of poems, and those from *Frontier Signals*, were collected in *Map of Clay*, Methuen, 1961, and form the foundation of his work. Indeed, these poems constitute about a third of the c150 pages of his Bloodaxe *Selected Poems* of 1988, based as they are on the clay-pit, clay-world, experience and, in a good many cases, allied to structural ability of the highest order, harnessing the 'gusto' of emotion and idea through rhythm, rhyme, and a consistent imagery, often drawn from his Calvinist inheritance, whether welcomed or not. In *Clay Cuts* (1991) he approved the reprinting of some of these poems with Stan Dobbins' woodcuts, but not the magnificent 'A Calvinist in Love' with which the Bloodaxe selection, like the Clemo section of *Penguin Modern Poets, 6*, 1964, opens:

> ...
> 'This bare clay-pit is truest setting
>   For love like ours:
>   No bed of flowers
> But sand-ledge for our petting. ...
>
> We cannot fuse with fallen Nature's
>   Our rhythmic tide:
>   It is allied
> With laws beyond the creatures. ...
>
> Our love is full-grown Dogma's offspring,
>   Election's child,
>   Making the wild
> Heats of our blood an offering.'

The eschewing of indulgence, natural lushness or ease in favour of something severe, ordered, yet an acknowledgement of grace, is extremely consistently and elegantly put before us here, whether we warm to it or not as a basis for living or belief. It is a form of *kenosis* or self-limitation, after the example of God-incarnate. Or rather, as Davie puts it, commenting on the related worship, with its 'simplicity, sobriety, and measure', we have not so much the denial of sensuous pleasure as sensuous pleasure of a particularly frugal and fastidious kind.[8] As to Calvinism itself – which emphasises the gift of Divine grace, election and predestination, as opposed to the free-will of Arminian theology, and the need of this gift by natural 'fallen' man, who cannot of himself 'earn' or 'merit' this restitution – I like what Davie says in another place, namely, that the intellectual vindication of Calvinism by Jonathan Edwards 'has never been controverted', 'but in the last hundred years or so 'has for the most part been tacitly laid aside, as experimentally unacceptable to the worshipper in the act of private devotion or public worship.'[9] As Malcolm Furness reminds us: we all tend to be Arminians in the pulpit, Calvinists on our knees.[10] 'The Plundered Fuchsias' (*Map of Clay*, 26-27 and ref.*40*, below) illustrates the lengths to which Clemo could take his austere, 'post-material' interpretation of Calvinism at this period. Yet ever and again it is this taut union of feeling and faith (or ' belief-emotion') which, when under rigorous formal control, gives the best poems of this period their authority and force. (cf.refs.*27-29*)

The structure of 'A Calvinist in Love' is in itself a model of its theological ideal. For one thing there is the firm, uncompromising structure, the outer longer lines rhyming and the two inner shorter lines rhyming, thus giving us an extremely lyrical ABBA pattern, reminiscent of that used by Tennyson in 'In Memoriam.' For another thing, the effect is terse, spare even, and not only in the inner lines, but in the overall effect of stanza and poem. For a third thing, the language of Calvinistic theology, such as 'election' is interwoven with an equally logical setting forth of the imagery Clemo the poet experienced: the 'clayworkdune-light', the 'bare clay-pit', the 'sand-ledge', the 'truculent gale', with an exactness and economy worthy of Housman. The several hyphenated couplings, suggestive of Browning, seem to me to work perfectly well and unobtrusively in the context of this poem. The word 'petting' is a little dated though its use presents no problem. Familiar as it was in the 1940s and '50s, the *Shorter OED* dates it to 1925.

The music of the verse, which reminds us of the major Victorians as well as of Hardy and Housman, is thus a skeleton dependent on a rigid backbone of logic. It is as metaphysical as Donne but with a greater clarity and simplicity, arguably. The reserve of the form serves the reserve of the poet, and contributes to an artefact created not to deny ardour or 'sensuous pleasure' but to affirm it in a highly formal and restrained, 'frugal' manner of the utmost 'fastidiousness.' How a poet acquires the skill for such work – whether from his own inspiration, study and experiment alone, the example of predecessors or association with co-workers such as Causley, in this case, at one point – is a process of the creative imagination that contains both common features and others unique to the individual case. How *does* the creative daemon choose the host to whom it will be tenant? What provides the motivating energy, gives the zest, the tooling ambition, and directs it to the making of a poem? Early as the poem comes in his *career*, Clemo was 35 by the year of *The Clay Verge* but had not yet lost his sight completely.

The only fact we have is the artefact, and a vintage offering of 'simplicity, sobriety, measure' is poured us in this poem – even if it is a deceptive simplicity which can obscure (as with any such poetry) the intensity of the poet's response that gave the breath of life or 'gusto' to it. What a paradox it is that this embanking or concentration increases the intrinsic force of a poem even as it appears to constrict it. This is true, of course, wherever structure controls emotion in a poem and what we see in the best poems is a tested (if unique) structure harnessing the strongest force. In a poet like Hopkins, the utmost energy is controlled in a highly complex, if austerely formal fashion. In Clemo's best work, a deceptively undemanding simplicity harnesses the force, though not all the poems are as ambitious as 'A Calvinist in Love'. That these poems are accessible does not mean that they are 'tossed off', far from it.

The vivid, evocative couplets of 'Snowfall at Kernick' may remind us of De La Mare, for he too is a deceptively mellifluous and accessible craftsman. 'The Water-Wheel', likewise, may strike us as Georgian, but if so the association must be seen as a two-way compliment. These poems, like 'The Flooded Clay-Pit', are concerned with their specific clay-pit imagery and mood, and this alone would give them distinction. 'Neutral Ground' is closer to 'A Calvinist in Love' in ambition, though its mood is altogether different; much more Hardyesque:

'God's image was washed out of Nature
    By the flood of the Fall ...

Not in Nature or God must my vision
    Now find some relief ...

I will turn to a world that is ravaged,
    Yet not by His Will,
A world whose derision of Nature
    Is rigid and shrill.

I have lost all the sensitive, tender,
    Deep insights of man:
I will look round a claywork in winter,
    And note what I can.'

So he sets out his manifesto. It is a touch didactic but there is (as in 'A Calvinist in Love') the spine of a clear mind at the centre of it. The poet has made his decision. The harsh clay world at his door will give him his subject. Un-stanzaic, less concise and formal poems, such as 'Christ in the Clay-Pit' or the lengthy 'The Excavator', revert to the Passion imagery behind 'A Calvinist ...', but are sprawling compared with his best poems. Rhyme is present but in arbitrary paragraphs and line-lengths such as Patmore, in his *The Unknown Eros* odes, and Henley, in his *London Voluntaries*, use with equally varying success. Yet there is no denying that many passages have considerable power:

'Just splintered wood and nails
Were fairest blossoming for Him Who speaks
Where mica-silt outbreaks
Like water from the side of His own clay ...'
                    ('Christ in the Clay-Pit')

or: 'The bars now hinged o'erhead and drooping form
       A Cross that lacks the symmetry
       Of those in churches, but is more

15

Like His whose stooping tore
The vitals from our world's foul secrecy.'
('The Excavator')

But when such paragraphs extend to any length they can run into
buffers of turgidity. Edwin Muir, in whose equally original work there
are similar moods and musings, likewise does better, I think, in his
structured, lyrical poems than in his more prosy, didactic manner,
though this may be a matter of taste.

The Wintry Priesthood sequence (1951) contains the same mixture of
lyrical and 'rhymed paragraph' pieces in the Patmore-ode mode. Two
of the more structured pieces stand out: 'Clay-Land Moods' with its
three 11-lined stanzas: 'Here on the sharp clay-tip there broods/Olympian
thunder'; and a poem of response to a fellow author, 'A Kindred
Battlefield', written early in 1950. It led to a visit Clemo made that
summer to the Dorset village of Mappowder to meet the reclusive author
of *Mr Weston's Good Wine*, T F Powys (1875-1953). It is interesting that
Clemo should have felt an affinity with Powys's brooding mixture of
earthy dualism and pious nihilism, which could produce the unrelieved
ironies of *Fables* and similar if more searing work, beside the moving
if dark 'The Only Penitent', and the mellow benignity of 'Come and
Dine', as well as *Mr Weston*, that masterpiece of compassionate
imagination, when one would have thought his own basic optimism[11]
would have accorded better with John Cowper Powys's much more
expansive and celebratory oeuvre; yet in 1978 he was to make a further
visit to Mappowder to see T F Powys's grave, a visit which he records
in 'Mappowder Revisited.' *Marriage of a Rebel* , 54-63 answers my
questions, in so far as they relate to T F Powys. Clemo responded to
Soliloquies of a Hermit, for one thing, whilst Powys's writing and
isolation (East Chaldon and Mappowder) paralleled his own feelings of
hermithood. Both authors use the familar terrain of their daily existence
for allegory, symbol or setting.[12]

In 'A Kindred Battlefield', something of Hardy and Housman may
underlie subject or method, yet there is the same beautiful clarity and
consistency of working out that distinguishes 'A Calvinist in Love': ...

'A labyrinth, a maze.
   Each chalky Dorset lane:
No landmark steadfast stays
   To guide the questing brain.

The baffling hedge of thorns,
   The swirling mist and sea,
The goblin world that scorns,
   Fret you continually. ...

The homely Stour may tame
   Terrors of Madder Hill,
The new earth name the Name -
   My clay-world feel the thrill. ...'

'The Two Beds' is dedicated to D H Lawrence and considers 'clay-bed' and 'coal-bed' in the light of 'the Man who died' who, says Clemo, 'is not as you supposed.' The dedication underlines the growing width of Clemo's literary sympathies and self-cultivation[13], spurred by his innate positiveness; the early stimulus of Browning, Donne, Spurgeon, and biographies of men like C T Studd. Karl Barth was to reinforce his faith and D H Lawrence the artistic potential of feeling. In 1958 he published *The Invading Gospel*, in which he emphasised his belief in the efficacy of Divine grace as opposed to human merit – not that he relaxed his own efforts, human, creative, or spiritual! – and in the take-over of the natural world by that grace. He seems to have seen in the glaring, often dazzling spread of the clay tips over his birth-scape an image of Heaven's take-over in action, and a visionary foretaste of the glory beckoning the disciple in and beyond this life.

In 1960 he was awarded a Civil List Pension, following an unsuccesful application in 1950, for which Derek Parker 'campaigned', supported by Charles Causeley, T F Powys, Aldous Huxley and Howard Spring, amongst others.[14]

Poems from 'Frontier Signals' in the 1961 *Map of Clay* volume include 'Goonvean Claywork Farm', dedicated to his patient and trustful mother, Eveline; 'Tregerthen Shadow', another piece dedicated to D H Lawrence; 'Intimate Landscape', in which Divine and earthly desire is combined and - as often with St John of the Cross - there is ambiguity as to who is being addressed ... but see *Marriage of a Rebel*, pp.27-29. 'Max Gate' is dedicated to Thomas Hardy, and 'Daybreak in Dorset' makes a number of allusions to Hardy and one to T F Powys's Mappowder. It is interesting to compare these (comparatively) early responses to 'literary' Dorset[15] with poems such as 'Dorset Roots' and 'Fleet' in the *Approach to Murano* collection of 1993, written much later in his life, and the mention in his correspondence of 1990 of Fielding, J Meade Falkner, and Browning's forebears, in addition to T F Powys and Hardy.[16]

By 1961, when *Map of Clay* was published, Clemo was 45 and already showing signs of a broader, more ecumenical engagement as in 'Beyond Lourdes' dedicated to St Bernadette. His *Cactus on Carmel* collection of 1967 builds on this in poems such as 'Carmel' and 'The Riven Niche', the latter again dedicated to Bernadette.

Cactus on Carmel reveals the increasing liberation of his thought from the clay-tip dominated world of the *Clay Verge* poems, by which he was still physically surrounded. It was a development that would culminate (poetically) in *The Echoing Tip* and *Broad Autumn* collections but ultimately range furthest (in the topographical sense) in those poems of Florence and the Venetian Lagoon which constituted the outward sign of an inner warming and, not least, a psychological homing for one whose lifelong literary impetus (after his faith and personal imperatives) had been Browning.

The work of his middle and later periods shows this constant broadening in subject matter, setting, and sympathy. His confidence and sense of self-identitity continues to strengthen, and the range of his references and subject-interests makes its own point. His mastery of the *dramatic monologue*, too, dates (in my view) from his middle and late fifties. *Stylistically*, development is more restrained, save for the growing predominance of arbitrary paragraph structures in the Patmore/ Henley tradition over lyrical work, and the winning of freedom from any initial stiffness or derivative gestures - though there is little of that in the earlier lyric work retained in the *Selected Poems* of 1988. Clemo does not radically alter his style at different periods of his career or to deal with particular moods, influences or themes innovatively and empathetically as do Pound, Eliot, Yeats, and Hughes, or the Dutch experimentalists of the 1950s, amongst others.[17]

He knows who and what he is. He is his own man. He sticks to his own manner, like a De la Mare or a Housman and, time and again, an outstanding poem breaks surface.

'Lunar Pentecost' is one such lyric in *Map of Clay*. It is an innovative integration of familiar, bleak yet moon-transformed landscape, vibrant with the active presence of Godhead, and that jazz and ragtime impetus to which his correspondence alludes.[18]

The few lyrics in *Cactus on Carmel* are equally restrained. The triplets of 'Gulls Nesting Inland' have a descriptive simplicity, yet we find it is the human condition as well as that of the birds which is under observation. 'Bedrock' starts with an abandoned stone mill yet ends with the mind's mill active, the blood exulting in discovery. It is after the mind has been 'sealed and rusted' that: ...

> 'The unbarred instinct is struck by grace
> As a playful hand lifts the bramble
> From my blind groping face.' ...

See the end of 'Mould of Castile' for a similar reference, and *Marriage of a Rebel*, 114-115, for the background.

'Bunyan's Daughter' and 'Friar's Crag' (to John Ruskin) indicate the constantly widening, if commonly literary and/or place based, range of his *subjects*. 'Dungeon Ghyll', 'Grasmere Reflections' and 'Lines to Wordsworth' arise from the visit to Lakeland that he reports on in *Marriage of Rebel* and that led to 'Friar's Crag'. 'Charlotte Nicholls', one of several poems he wrote over the years on the Bronte family, concerns the author of *Jane Eyre*.

In the autumn of 1990 he was to comment: 'Nearly all my poems in recent years have stemmed from holiday visits to various places - an odd contrast to my early phase in which I could compose poems only when stuck in a clay-pit.'[19] His *themes* continue to be those of his physical and mental terrain: the dialogue with God; the emotional and spiritual pilgrimage. Yet how striking is the objectivity and comparative balance of his approach, especially given the frustrations of his particular circumstances.

II By the time *The Echoing Tip* was published in 1971 there had been a significant event. On Saturday, 26th October, 1968, in Trethosa chapel, Jack Clemo and Ruth Peaty were married. Ruth (and her sister Bella) hailed from Weymouth in Dorset. She was of Brethren upbringing and, like Jack, a Gospel-oriented person.[20] Her work had been in a laundry and, like Jack's, her education owed much to herself. Her reading included such authors as Aquinas, Jung and Kierkegaard. On their marriage they lived in the Goonamarris cottage – with Jack's mother, Eveline, until her death in 1977 – with the clay-workings besieging the cottage till every walk and view was compromised and the very route to their home diverted. In earlier years such things as the rope-hauled tip wagons had had a certain poetry about them, but changing methods must have made the life for Ruth, who was not used to it, and was not handicapped, a 'depressing and soul-deadening' experience.[21] It was to be 1984, however, before the couple left Goonamarris and settled down in the Peaty family home in Rodwell, Weymouth, with its steps to the front door and closeness to sea and beach, where they were to live so happily.

Each was fortunate in the understanding, forbearance and wisdom that they found in the other, and Ruth – as, when necessary, Bella – was unstinting in her care. There was nothing that Clemo came to like more than a paddle on Sandsfoot Beach, and the atmosphere of their home, where he had his desk and work-place in the living room, was calm, cheerful and welcoming.

In 1970 he was crowned Poet of Clay at the Cornish Gorsedd Festival at Perranporth.

In 1971, when *The Echoing Tip* appeared, he was 55. In it he reveals his growing mastery of his mentor Browning's metier, the dramatic monologue. It is no surprise that 'Helen Keller at Wrentham' is a telling and empathetic monologue, given the relevance to Clemo's own situation. But the protagonist of 'Mary Shelley in Geneva' (nee Godwin and author of *Frankenstein*) cites Harriet Westbrook, Byron, Claire Clairmont, her husband and 'The grim sea fumbling at our castle walls', Plato, Sophocles and Calvin, with a like ease of manner. In connection with Calvin see other poems in *The Echoing Tip*' such as 'After Billy Bray' and 'On the Death of Karl Barth', and discussion above of the early 'A Calvinist in Love'. After mention of Harriet, in the present poem, Mary says:

> 'Is there only a search,
> Through snow or water-beds, for one's true self
> Or a loved one's self, decayed, repulsive, lost?'

In the marvellously vivid 'Alfred Wallis' monologue he captures the vital essence of the Cornish fisherman-cum-Sally Army-revivalist-cum-unschooled artist who painted late in life and ended up in the workhouse – but not before inspiring people as diverse as Ben Nicholson, Christopher Wood and, very evidently, Clemo.[22] 'William Blake Notes a Demonstration', set in London' is another indication both of his skill with the dramatic monologue and the creative zest provided by his marriage.[23]

Further evidence of the happy influence of his marriage is to be found in two of the most lyrically structured poems in the collection. One is 'Wedding Eve' (to Ruth) in eight 6-lined rhyming stanzas:

> 'Chrysanthemums scent the empty chapel
> On this last night of my unpartnered bed ...'

> Elect for marriage – I sang
> That stubborn theme through three decades
> Of hunger, mirage, avalanche:
> When nature made hopes blanch,
> A text like a clay-bed tang,
> Like the bride's own breath, stirred in the shades ...

> And we find how disenchanted seed
> Is changed to spirit's Cana-spark.'

The other is 'The Brownings at Vallombrosa', the title of which calls up Milton's: 'Thick as autumnal leaves that strow the brooks/In Vallombrosa', as well as that poet and that union which had sustained and inspired Clemo over so many years. How fitting it is that he should have written these quatrains at this juncture and have set it close to the 'Wedding Eve' poem:

> 'Lyric currents plough though them,
> Natural as the wild Apennine streams ...'

> But back at the Calvinist chapel
> Their subtlest love has leaned to dogma's air:
> After the doubts and the maturing grapple
> Came the romantic arbiter ...

> A rebel grace that marks
> The Puritan juncture at which both are freed.'

The initial poem of the collection, 'I go gentle', sees Clemo taking issue with Dylan Thomas's well known poem to his dying father. In *Marriage of a Rebel*, however, he says that Thomas and T S Eliot, 'these two 'modern rebels', are more congenial to him than 'neat traditionalists.'[24]

Donald Davie's admiration for 'Mould of Castile' (to St Teresa) has already been noted,[25] together with the 'bramble' reference that recalls 'Bedrock.'

'A Nanpean Student', not included in the Bloodaxe *Selected Poems*, is a moving tribute to Sylvia Crowle, an Oxford student and Methodist local preacher, tragically killed in a car accident. (see Ref.5)

In 1973, Mrs Peaty, Ruth's mother died, after a difficult period that had left Ruth with divided loyalties. It is indicative of the impetus provided by Clemo's marriage, however, that *Broad Autumn*, which followed *The Echoing Tip* in 1975, proved to be in the same fertile vein. The lyrical and/or structured poems include 'Josephine Butler', 'A Night in Soho', 'A Young Mystic, II', 'Herman Melville', 'A Wife on an Autumn Anniversary', 'On the Burial of a Poet Laureate', and

'Wamba Convent 1964' which has a liturgical refrain. Amongst these 'Herman Melville' and 'Josephine Butler' are outstanding for their unifying command of imagery and idea, phrase and structure, and of 'voice' in the dramatic monologue. As 'Herman Melville' tells us:

'Ultimate claims a voice in me ...

That dark demented clash in remote waters
Faded in cold ambiguity:
Would Christ slay pride of doubt or pride of faith
Or pride of blood, or save, transform all three?'

This is a fine achievement and must rank amongst his best two dozen poems, together with 'Alfred Wallis' 'Bedrock', 'Lunar Pentecost', 'A Kindred Battlefied', 'A Calvinist in Love', and 'Josephine Butler', a *tour de force* in which the Victorian social reformer reflects in three 11-lined rhymed stanzas. It is colloquial, detailed, socially knowledgeable and compassionate, holds its content together, and works splendidly as a poem:

'God, why do I dare –
I, married and fifty – defy the established crime?'

The answer lies not only in her compassion and concern, and her innate personal qualities, but in the Christian belief that commissions her: her whole-hearted endeavour to see 'Christ's martyred love conquer', to quote the poem again. This raises an important point. Josephine Butler would not have been herself or done her work as she did, had she not been activated by her background and Christian belief. To deny this is to be false to her allegiance, its impetus, its enabling, and its effect.[26] It is the same with Clemo himself. His poetry and his faith are indivisible. You cannot divorce or ignore them. In this he is at one with Hopkins, whose devotion is such an intrinsic source and force in his work ... which is in no way to deny that with each poet this is bound up with corporeal emotions that are often intense. Some have regretted what they have seen as the restrictive effects of Hopkins' Jesuit priesthood. Others may not empathise with Clemo's beliefs or the abundant evidence of them that he gives us in his work. In each case, there is no getting round it. It is faith that gives force and spine to the work, as to the man; belief and devotion that determines its character. You cannot have the one without the other, and not to accept this and acknowledge it, is to be perversely unfaithful to one's subject.[27] It is the same with Newman[28,29] – who helped Hopkins at a critical moment - and countless others.[30]

Equally moving is Clemo's empathy with Donne in 'A Night in Soho':
...

'Only St Paul's, your intact stone
Tongue, chimed a post-war grace.
You hymned the whore's licence and the rake's bone,
Then blasted through to our time, to me in that place'

– or with his fellow craftsman C Day Lewis in 'On the Burial of a Poet Laureate': ...

'I could join you there in the discovery
That the resinous craft,
Pure form, needs inward friction, the soul bowed, searching
      ... crosstree,
Grail-blood, the cosmic graft.

You told me once my firm and clarion metres
Suspended your disbelief ...'

In 'Wart and Pearl' Clemo shows his empathy with Hopkins, one of the few poets whose faithful fervour, kept under such rigorous (even austere) control, could be seen as intenser (if arguably narrower) than his own. Clemo is surely right in seeing an affinity between his own austere, if gusty, Calvinistic Nonconformity with the gusto of certain of the Catholic saints or this devout Jesuit priest. Even so, there is some distancing, some limit to empathy, in this poem.

'The Harassed Preacher' is dashing and beautifully shaped, with a 'chorus' that shows other sides of ideas, and sends thought in different

24

directions, like a set of mirrors or a scatter-gun. As a veteran of these chapels with their 'five villagers', I find it moving. The related 'John Wesley' is equally well worked. Its six taut ten-lined rhymed stanzas convey the mental experience and the intellectual/emotional make-up of the great proselytiser in vivid, integrated images and 'the rivets of à Kempis.' In the four verses of 'Comeley Bank'(sic), Clemo muses on marriage, trusting that, through regard and prayer, he can improve on the earnest yet sad example of Thomas and Jane Welsh Carlyle – taking the received view of their life together, which is perhaps not its only truth. 'Comley Bank', Edinburgh, as Thomas spelt it, was the Carlyles' first home.

'Helpston' is about John Clare. 'In Harlyn Museum', offers flints and a female skull. Its mood and subject recall Eric Ratcliffe and Seamus Heaney. 'Testament' is dedicated to Clemo's much older cousin, the Cornish novelist and Methodist minister, Joseph Hocking, 1855-1937, himself a tin-miner's son.[31] 'Wessex and Lyonesse' refers to T F Powys and Hardy. 'Whispers' makes at least one reader think of Edwin Muir and C H Sisson:

> 'These whispers must come from ahead,
> From a point where the road bends round
> Into faith-flushed terrain again,
> Beyond the last factory-shed
> Of secular mirage.' ...

'St Gildas' is in tribute to Alexis Carrel 1873-1944, the Nobel prize winning physiologist. In 'Royal Wedding' Clemo speaks of marriage as he understands it and of the Abbey or 'oasis' where 'Bones of great lovers lie', 'Browning and Tennyson' amongst them, viewed from Goonamarris.

In 1977, Eveline Clemo, Jack's mother, died. In 1980 *Marriage of a Rebel* was published [an augmented edition appeared in 1988], and his early life was the subject of a BBC documentary entitled 'A Different Drummer.' In the following year, Exeter University awarded him an honorary D Litt. degree. His humorous dialect stories and 'light' verse appeared in *The Bouncing Hills* in 1983 – though an evocative poem like 'Slag Vision' certainly asks to be taken seriously. The book also contains a small glossary of the Cornish dialect. In 1984 he and Ruth moved to Rodwell, Weymouth,[32] where he worshipped at the Baptist Church.

III Not too many people have their second novel published in their seventieth year, but 1986 saw the publication of *The Shadowed Bed*, of which Clemo writes:

'I think it's my best *imaginative presentation* of Christianity as well as my strongest evocation of the Cornish clay landscape and the sort of villagers I knew before I was handicapped. This type of novel isn't popular, but I don't feel I wasted those years in writing it .'[33]

It was written soon after the Second World War, around the time that *Wilding Graft* was published.

A Different Drummer was published in 1986, the same year as *The Shadowed Bed*. There are some thirty-six poems in the collection, only nine of which are included in the Bloodaxe *Selected Poems*. Amongst the poems not chosen by Bloodaxe are pieces on Charlotte Mew, Gladys Aylward, Virginia Woolf[34], Francis Thompson, Holman Hunt, Eric Gill, Thomas Hardy ('Hardy's Birthplace', a well-crafted response to simplicity and the rural quiet of Bockhampton),and Dietrich Bonhoeffer. The poem to Oswald Chambers, 'A Choice About Art', I would certainly like to have seen included. It contrasts Chambers' choice, preaching rather than art, with Van Gogh's (ultimate) choice, art rather than preaching. It is a telling job, in six 6-lined rhymed stanzas, even if one's heart might still be with Van Gogh:

'Choice of the Kingdom Van Gogh had seen
But let slip for the sun's
Rank relish for colour ...

The pulpit had lost a voice, the galleries gained
Some savage pictures. Fate must respond
To a man's choice ...'

Of the nine Bloodaxe choices, the more structured poems are 'Jim Elliot', and 'In a Truro Garden', in which '...a petal lifts/ Rough and spongy...'. It is a beautifully simple, evocative poem. 'Jim Elliot' is an altogether tougher, more ambiguous piece, its pulse harnessed in quatrains rhyming ABBA. Jim Elliot was an American missionary murdered in Ecuador in 1956.

> '... tough as Hemingway,
> He saw life stripped and God-raided ...
> Religion-less faith, more radical than Bonhoeffer's,
> Blazed its challenge through his hard grip ...
> "The secular is sacred enough ..." ...
> In the sweating jungle of Ecuador ...
> Objective mandate checking his flaw ...'

In 'Poem at Sixty' Clemo compares his own experience of succouring grace to Paul's conversion on the Damascus Road, as he thinks of fellow authors – Chatterton, Mew, Davidson, Vachel Lindsay, and others – who have taken their lives. 'In Roche Church' vigorously conjures its hill-scape, yet ends in affecting reminiscence of two Philip Larkin poems.[35]

'Mappowder Revisited' inevitably recalls his earlier poem 'A Kindred Battlefield' and his visit of 1950, as it recounts his 1978 visit with Ruth to the grave of T F Powys.[36]

'Sandsfoot Castle Gardens' – Sandsfoot being the beach where Clemo loved to paddle in his Weymouth years – and 'Chesil Beach' make a topgraphically related pair. In the 'Sandsfoot' poem he contrasts the scene with the clay-fields and ponders:

> '...the cruel fate distorting clay-fields and me ...'

The 1988 *Selected Poems* ends with three poems that appear five years later in *Approach to Murano*, as a result of his visit to Venice with Ruth in October 1987. 'Palazzo Rezzonico' responds to the 17th & 18th century palace (latterly housing an art collection) where Browning was to die and Whistler stay for a few months. In 'Jean-Pierre de Caussade' his subject is a religious who went blind 'at seventy or so'. Back home, in 'Open Waters', he comes full circle: ...

'I think of another dimension -
A Dissent hub on a Weymouth quay,
An open baptistry, wet hair on my cheek;
And I touch the unquenched praise
Believers have always smuggled
Into a world ever menaced, yet intact. ...'

August 1989 saw the publication of *Banner Poems*, 'minor descriptive verse' Clemo had contributed to the "Cornish Banner", ironically, he felt, in view of his 'strictures on Cornish nationalism in *Confession of a Rebel*'.[37] *Clay Cuts*, a Previous Parrot Press publication of 1991 (14th January 1992) featured a selection of his earlier 'clay-land' poems with woodcuts by Stan Dobbin.[38]

IV In *Approach to Murano*, 1993, and the posthumous *The Cured Arno* of 1995, we have what can be considered the last, and fourth, stage of his work. This is if we regard the clay-world up to his marriage as the first stage (though this could be subdivided into pre-recognition and post-recognition spheres, or take account of his advance, or retreat, from his intense response to belief in the context of a single setting and image source), his life at Goonamarris with Ruth to 1984 as the second, and the years between 1984 and *Murano* as the third, for it seems to me that the Italian visits, in the footsteps of his lifelong inspiration, Browning, coincided with warmer, widening sympathies and a great sense of Providential benignity, even if, for the most part, critics[39,40] consider his best work, technically speaking, to have been behind him. The impetus came from the visit with Ruth to Venice, and the 'model gondola made of Murano glass' that Ruth brought back with her to England, which became for him a symbol of his 'spiritual journey from clay to glass.'[41] By Whitsun, 1991, Clemo was 'cheered' by Bloodaxe's acceptance of the *Murano* book, and he seems to have looked forward to its publication with exceptional anticipation. The more therefore was he disappointed when its appearance was delayed until March 1993, as his letters show.[42] Prior to its appearance he had published a 'very short account' of the Venetian visit, with photographs, in the January, 1990, issue of *Christian Woman*.[43] From this it is clear that we shall not look in vain for autobiographical elements or parallels with Browning in the collection.

The first poem, 'The Model', explains the background. The gondola is: 'Modestly harboured where my pen glides'. The concluding poem, 'Ring and Pen', has Clemo losing and finding the pen Ruth had given him as an engagement present and recalling the ring the Doge once cast into the sea as a token of the serene republic's marriage to it, a subject to which 'Island Contrasts' and 'San Lazzaro' also allude. In 'Palazzo Rezzonico' (mentioned above): 'the unclayed body/ Boarded a gondola at Venice,' while the poems 'Venice', 'A Slant from St Mark's', 'Late Honeymoon', further paint his response to what is one of cultural Europe's most reverberating settings.

> 'Give me the Doges' symbol, the marriage-ring
> Cast with the grave exultant ritual
> Into the Adriatic. She is still wedded,
> My rich city, to the sanctioned tongued sea.
> I have thrilled to the ordered heaving
> Near the nuptial fresco that drew Browning
> From Camberwell ...'

he says in 'San Lazzaro', whilst 'Festal Magnet' confirms and honours his earliest and most vital literary affection once more:

> 'I did not climb through the cloud barrier
> To track these dark phantoms, but to contact
> The soil and climate in which my faith
> First reached into poetry, rich with Italian colour
> Through Browning's pen. My Cornish images
> Of smoke, iron and gravel
> Stirred later on my drab fate's level ...'

There are Dorset poems in the collection: 'Dorset Roots', 'William Barnes' and 'Fleet' which recall 'A Kindred Battlefield', 'Max Gate' and 'Daybreak in Dorset' of thirty to forty years earlier.[44] He was 'a Dorset townsman'[45] by then, of course, as his correspondence of 1990 reflects.[46]

'Hudson Taylor' is a fine, characteristic poem, in his rhyming, stanzaic mode. Its dedicated ambiguity (and humanity) is in the 'Jim Elliot', 'A Choice about Art' (to Oswald Chambers), and 'Herman Melville' mould. It is a theme to which his whole nature responds, and which thus finds him at his best. A related, if lighter, piece is on 'The Kilns', the house near Oxford where C S Lewis lived. It ends with a touching play on the 'Narnia' author's late love (and wife) Joy's name: 'Joy still hunts/ For surprises, teasing after the grave sting.'[47]

In September 1993, Clemo paid his second and last visit to Italy, which was to fructify in *The Cured Arno*, published after his death. He and Ruth saw Venice again and also went to Florence and Pisa.

Jack Clemo died in Dorchester hospital on the 25th July 1994. The funeral service was held at Weymouth Baptist Church, which he and Ruth had attended, and he is buried in Weymouth cemetery. But this did not mean that his output had ceased.

The Cured Arno appeared posthumously in 1995, but had been clearly envisaged and projected by Clemo, as the Author and Publishers[48] and John Hurst[49] make clear. It stems from the visit Ruth and Jack made in September 1993. In Clemo's Prefatory Note he refers to the river being 'cured' of its 'erratic and treacherous behaviour' which led to 'destructive winter floods and the stench of its dry bed in summer'. It was an image apt for his purpose, he felt, whether in the context of the loss of the *Titanic*, which indicated the fallibility of the philosophy of material progress, or of his 'late marriage' which he says 'cured my warped and bleak isolationism.'[50] Together with *Approach to Murano* it completes the psychological curve initiated by this clay-Calvinist's response to Browning, and with the poem 'Quenched', rounds off his career with a particular appropriateness. It is not necessarily the culmination of his work, which is to be found, in my judgement, within *The Echoing Tip* and *Broad Autumn* collections, published in 1971 and 1975, when he was in his 'fifties, following the earlier 'Calvinist/ clay world' achievements collected in *The Map of Clay*.

As we might expect there are abundant references to the Brownings in the collection[51]; not least to Casa Guidi on the Piazza San Felice, the

Brownings' Florentine home.[52] 'The Tower' initiates us with references to Florence and the Arno, Casa Guidi, and:

'... Browning's last whim,
Planning a tower, a Pippa memorial
High on the crest of Asolo,
The town of silkmills ...'.

In 'Fever Zone' he climbs the 'breezy hills of Vallombrosa', reminding us of his 'The Brownings at Vallombrosa', written more than twenty years earlier. 'Headway' treats of Florence and Pisa, but ends with the human condition:

'But the heart stays vulnerable, in flux,
Or prone to an off-centre pull.'

'Casa Guidi' has a poem to itself. The study, drawing room, 'clinging fresco' seem 'potent' with:

'... the vibrant magic that pierced me in Cornwall
With my first Browning page, read in crisis. ...'

In 'Heretic in Florence', the closing poem, again he thinks of Casa Guidi where: 'The Brownings fused aesthete and Puritan' in that city where now: 'The cured Arno sings in freedom.'
'Journey North' describes his and Ruth's train journey from Florence to Venice and the Lagoon.
There are further poems on the Brontes: 'Ann Bronte'[53] and 'Foreign Idiom', in which he sees parallels between his own upbringing and that of the Brontes, and comes back to Casa Guidi as counterpoise. The poems on Dorset include 'Stourhead' with its autobiographical element:

'The only Dorset river
I ever looked at splits near me
Confused by the row of rooted arches
At Sturminster ...'

This is aptly described – and remembered – while how keenly, yet with disarming restraint, he recalls the 'Lake Paddle' experienced near Keswick:

> 'We do not deal with tides: the lake shore
> Intones no flattery or withdrawal. ...'

'Growing in Grace' is a very unusual poem (for Clemo). It is a terse imagist piece, far-Eastern in its succinct clarity.[54] It is interesting to relate this poem to (say) 'The Plundered Fuchsias' of *The Map of Clay* or the late 'clay' poems in this, his last collection. With these poems on the clay–scape that was his life until 1968, in one sense, and 1984, in another – the impact of which never quite left him – he comes full circle. In 'Wheal Martyn' he writes of that once glaring and clanking clay-working which had, first, modernised itself from what he and his forebears experienced and, then, closed and become part of this country's industrial archaeology or museum culture. 'Modern methods', he concludes in the poem, 'lay no track of pipeway for my song.' Yet a letter of 1992, indicates his pleasure at his MSS and memorabilia being added to the 'newly started Clemo collection' there.[55]

The publishers explain that the poem 'Quenched' appears separately in the series of notebooks that contain *The Cured Arno* poems, and followed a visit that Clemo made with Ruth to his old cottage at Goonamarris in May, 1994, a few weeks before his death. 'Tip-flare, pit-spurt, tank-twinkle' have gone. 'The switches are still and unused .../No current jabs.'

> 'The clay fantasy blazed around my cottage
> When I last slept there. ...
> But I avoid the house now:
> Its dark night has no message for me.'

But Jack Clemo, triumphant survivor as man and poet, blazed out his faith and his fantasy, and leaves his message for us all.

[Brian Louis Pearce, Twickenham, 2001]

32

References

1   Letter of JC to BLP, 5th April 1989.
2   Davie, Donald *Dissentient Voice*, 1982, 48-56, 58, (52-55); see also *A Gathered Church*: the literature of the English Dissenting Interest, 1700-1930, 1978, for its general interest as its cut-off date precludes Clemo.
3   Gay, J D *The Geography of Religion in England*, 1971, 148-9, 159-167 (159-162), 303-311, 315 6 (Maps 37-45, 49-50), for Cornish and Calvinist Methodism.
4   Letter of JC to BLP, 17th July 1989.
5   *Methodist Recorder*, 4th August 1994
6   *Journal, URC History Society*, Vol.3, No.9, October 1986, 368-376
7   Pearce, B L 'Thoughts on Being a Nonconformist Aesthete', *Reformed Quarterly*, Vol.3, No.3, Oct/Nov 1992, 6-8, for reference to Jenkins, Davie, and *en passant* Clemo. For the full revised text of this essay see pp.79-86 of the present book.
8   Davie, D *A Gathered Church*, 1978, 25-26
9   op.cit., 11-12
10 Furness, M *Vital Doctrines of the Faith*, 1973, 63-64
11 Letter of JC to BLP, 2nd April 1991: 'He (Browning) remains the only great poet who presents my blend of mysticism, realism and optimism!'
12 Cf. the poem 'The Powder and the Spark' for the author's response to Mappowder's associations.
13 An apotheosis of the Protestant work-ethic and self-help given Clemo's or Lawrence's early circumstances.
14 Clemo, Jack *Marriage of a Rebel*, 1980, 113
15 Legg, Rodney *Literary Dorset*, 1990
16 Letters of JC to BLP, 27th June and 18th September 1990
17 Cf. the present writer's *Jack o'Lent*, 1991, influenced by the paintings of Francis Bacon; *Office Hours*, 1983; and 'Easter' sequence, influenced by Surrealist and Cubist art, in *Selected Poems 1951-1973*, 1977
18 See Ref.1
19 Letter of JC to BLP, 10th September 1990
20 Coad, R *A History of the Brethren Movement*, 2nd ed., 1976, 75; By coincidence Margaret Pearce (nee Wood) was Brethren before marriage.
21 *Marriage of a Rebel*, 148
22 op.cit., 138; and Letter of JC to BLP, 5th April 1989
23 Letter of JC to BLP, 11th December 1990
24 *Marriage of a Rebel*, 145
25 See Ref.2

26 Cf. Kenny, Mary 'It is Christianity that gave birth to Feminism', *Daily Telegraph*, 5.1.2001, 29 (What she says about the failure to acknowledge the Christian impetus behind social reformers like Josephine Butler is to the point.)

27 Pearce, B L *Varieties of Fervour*, 1996, 66-75 (lecture on Hopkins), 69

28 op.cit., 54-55 ('The Catholics'), 69

29 Pearce, B L 'The Idea of Newman and the Useful Arts', *Journal RSA*, CXXXVIII (5412), November 1990, 847-9

30 op.cit., 847 (note. 22, on John Clifford)

31 Another cousin was Joseph's brother Silas Kitto Hocking (1850-1935), also a preacher and a novelist. Cf. the *DNB* under Silas for both men. In 1950, when I joined the staff, the Borough Librarian of Acton, Middlesex, was Cornishman Charles Hocking, then about to retire. He was the author of a *Dictionary of Disasters at Sea during the age of steam, 1824-1962*, published by Lloyds Register of Shipping. Every morning he greeted each one of his staff personally. Once in an exam. room, when he was invigilating, he advanced down the long line of desks and called out 'Hello, Mr Pearce!', much to my consternation. *His* novelist daughter, Mary Hocking, FRSL, now lives in Lewes. The name is a common Cornish one, however, and Charles and Mary are not related to Joseph or Silas Kitto.

32 Cf. the present writer's poem 'At Rodwell.'

33 Letter of JC to BLP, 27th March 1990

34 Re Virginia Woolf, cf. letter of JC to BLP, 15th June 1993

35 'Church Going', and 'An Arundel Tomb' which ends: 'what will survive of us is love'.

36 Cf. the present writer's 'The Powder and the Spark' in response to T F Powys & Clemo, and a visit to Mappowder, made on 24th May 1993, recollected in December, 2000

37 Letter of JC to BLP, 27th March 1990

38 Letter of JC to BLP, 18th January 1992

39 Obituary, *Daily Telegraph*, 26th July 1994

40 Oxley, William, editor *Completing the Picture: exiles, outsiders and independents*, 1995, 43-47 (43-44)

41 Letter of JC to BLP, 15th August 1991

42 Letters of JC to BLP, 18th January and 16th July 1992, and 15th June 1993

43 Letter of JC to BLP, 27th March 1990

44 Other Dorset poems in *Approach to Murano* are 'At Cerne', 'Near the Race', 'The Split', 'Sunset in Dorset, and 'Tryphena'

45 Letter of JC to BLP, 5th April 1989

46   Letters of JC to BLP, 27th June and 10th September 1990

47   Letter of JC to BLP, 2nd April and postcard, c.10th April, 1991

48   *The Cured Arno*, 1995, [6] and [9], Publisher's and Author's Prefatory Note, respectively

49   Hurst, John 'Voice from a White Silence: the manuscripts of Jack Clemo' [in the Exeter University Library], *Jrnl. Inst. Cornish Studies*, Autumn, 1995, 125-143

50   Ref.48, p.[9]

51   Letters of JC to BLP, 2nd April 1991 and 18th January 1992

52   Cf. Eton College Library or The Browning Society for further details regarding Casa Guidi and/or The Friends of Casa Guidi

53   The poem relates to Ann Bronte's time with the Robinson family. [Her unassuming grave is clearly marked, near the castle in Scarborough]

54   'I proved thee ...' is a reference both to his mother Eveline's book *I Proved Thee at the Waters*, 1976, and to Psalm 81:7: 'Thou callest me in trouble and I delivered thee ... I proved thee at the waters of Meribah.' This poem was selected by Donald Davie for the *Oxford Book of Christian Verse*, 1982

55   Letter of JC to BLP, 16th July 1992

Clemo's People: an Introduction

1 The index that follows shows those writers and others with whom Clemo empathised most deeply and took as subjects for poems. In some cases there is the added interest of observing his treatment of or attitude toward a subject as he returned to it over many years. In many instances several persons are named within a poem, making for rich patterns of reference and association, if sometimes running the danger of obscuring the poetry in the web of nomenclature. Those writers of (or to) whom he writes most often are the Brontes, the Brownings, Hardy and T F Powys and, to a lesser extent, Byron, Bunyan, Melville and C S Lewis. Preachers and theologians include Calvin, Billy Bray, Spurgeon, Wesley, Karl Barth and Knox. St Bernadette comes first amongst the saints

It would not have been difficult to add a list of 'west country writers' but I came to doubt if the term was ultimately helpful or permitted of satisfactory definition. For one thing there are some authors who are deeply influenced by environment and/or stay in one place for decades. For others this is not so. Hardy, Barnes, Clemo himself and the Powys brothers, are amongst the few, I suspect, whose work is intrinsically shaped by, and part and parcel of, the area, though see, eg. JC's letter of 27th June, 1990.

2 Clemo's *dramatic monologues* stem, for the most part, from the years 1967 to 1986, when he was in his fifties and sixties, following his meeting with and marriage to Ruth Peaty. Thus they are most of them to be found in *Cactus on Carmel* 1967, *The Echoing Tip* 1971, *Broad Autumn* 1975, and *A Different Drummer* 1986. They peak, in my view, in *The Echoing Tip* and *Broad Autumn*, in poems such as 'Alfred Wallis', 'Josephine Butler' and 'Herman Melville', though in 'Hudson Taylor to Maria', in *Approach to Murano* 1993, he is as successful as ever. Among the stanzaic monologues[1], 'Wamba Convent' is unusual in having a refrain.[2]

3 This use of the dramatic monologue and interest in people of an earlier generation as subjects was the part fruit of a conscious decision, if logically pertinent process. Following his marriage he strove for 'objective portraiture', as he himself puts it in the prefatory note to *The Echoing Tip*, rather than confine himself to those personal emotions that

36

had predominated earlier. This he did both in the dramatic monologue and in his own voice, taking historical figures for his subjects far more than most poets[3] and frequently taking a subject's name as the title of his poem. It is indicative of his background and preoccupations that writers, preachers and missionaries should feature so largely amongst his favoured subjects, so that, though his 'gallery' is large, it has a remarkable coherence. Thus it is that in this genre, and especially in the dramatic monologue, he resembles his great mentor, Browning.

1 Stanzaic monologues are marked by an asterisk in the list that follows.
2 A purist might regret the extra line in the fourth stanza.
3 Though one cannot overlook Betjeman or, of contemporaries, Louis Hemmings, who corresponded with Clemo. Cf. Hemmings' *Firstborn*, Samovar Press, 1993

Clemo's People: Some Dramatic Monologues

The Clay-Tip Worker MOC *1961*

Bunyan's Daughter COC *1967*
Charlotte Nicholls COC

Mary Shelley in Geneva ET *1971*
Helen Keller at Wrentham ET[1]
Alfred Wallis ET
William Blake Notes a Demonstration ET
Katharine Luther ET[2]

Asian Girl in Mid-Cornwall BA *1975*
*The Harassed Preacher BA
*Josephine Butler BA
*Herman Melville BA
*Wamba Convent BA
*A Wife on an Autumn Anniversary BA

Charlotte Mew DD *1986*
Virginia Woolf Remembers St Ives DD
Holman Hunt DD
Henry Martyn DD
*Juan Diego DD
Eilidh Boadella (*in part*) DD

*Hudson Taylor to Maria ATM *1993*

1 The Helen Keller poem is telling in its own right as well as
   through its obvious links with Clemo's own situation.
2 'Mould of Castile', also from *The Echoing Tip*, is noteworthy
   for how close it gets to the *spirit* of the dramatic
   monologue without being one, by entering into how it
   felt (to the poet, at least) to *be* St Teresa.

Clemo's People: Persons as Subjects

Writers

Matthew Arnold	Dissenting Solo ATM
Florence Barclay	Florence Barclay DD
William Barnes	William Barnes ATM
T L Beddoes	Poem at Sixty DD
William Blake	William Blake Notes a Demonstration ET
Eilidh Boadella	Eilidh Boadella DD
The Brontes	Charlotte Nicholls COC/ Ste Gudule and St Agnes ET/ Salvaged DD/ Emily Bronte ATM/ Haworth Keys 1840 ATM/ Anne Bronte CA/ Foreign Idiom CA
E B & Robert Browning	Edward Barrett in Cornwall ET/ The Brownings at Vallombrosa ET/ A Couple at Fowey ET/ Royal Wedding BA/ Florence Barclay DD/ The Prospect of Leaving my Birthplace ATM/ Dorset Roots ATM/ Festal Magnet ATM/ Palazzo Rezzonico ATM/ San Lazzaro ATM/ Venice ATM/ Ring and Pen ATM/ The Tower CA/ Journey North CA/ Casa Guidi CA/ Foreign Idiom CA/ Heretic in Cornwall CA
John Bunyan	Bunyan's Daughter COC/ Link at Oxford ATM/ Morning Call CA
Robert Burns	Testament BA/ John Harris ATM
Byron	Mary Shelley in Geneva ET/ San Lazzaro ATM/ Silver Wedding CA/ Foreign Idiom CA
Jane & Thomas Carlyle	Comeley Bank BA
Charles Causley	Dedication to *The Echoing Tip* (book)/ Meeting-points ATM
Thomas Chatterton	Poem at Sixty DD
John Clare	Helpston BA/ John Harris ATM
Hart Crane	Poem at Sixty DD
e e Cummings	Schooling CA

Dante	Journey North CA/ Heretic in Florence CA
John Davidson	Poem at Sixty DD
John Donne	A Night in Soho BA
Caradoc Evans	Caradoc Evans DD
J M Falkner	Fleet ATM (by association)
Henry Fielding	Dorset Roots ATM/ Milton Abbey CA
Goethe	Dietrich Bonhoeffer DD
Thomas Hardy	Max Gate MOC/ Daybreak in Dorset MOC/ In Contrast ET/ Wessex and Lyonesse BA/ On the Burial of a Poet Laureate BA/ At Hardy's Birthplace DD/ Isle of Slingers DD/ Tryphena ATM/ William Barnes ATM/ Silver Wedding CA/ Dorchester Ward CA
John Harris	John Harris ATM
Ernest Hemingway	Jack London CA / Jim Elliot DD
Joseph Hocking	Testament BA
Homer	T E Lawrence CA
G M Hopkins	Wart and Pearl BA/ A Choice About Art DD
Victor Hugo	Silver Wedding CA
John Keats	In Contrast ET/ Eilidh Boadella DD/ George Muller CA
Helen Keller	Helen Keller at Wrentham ET
D H Lawrence	The Two Beds MOC/ Tregerthen Shadow MOC
T E Lawrence	T E Lawrence CA
C Day Lewis	On the Burial of a Poet Laureate BA
C S Lewis	Porth Beach (Ack.) BA/ Link at Oxford ATM/ The Kilns ATM
Vachel Lindsay	Poem at Sixty DD
Jack London	Jack London CA
Herman Melville	(Harpoon ET)/ Herman Melville BA/ Jack London CA
Charlotte Mew	Poem at Sixty DD/ Charlotte Mew DD
Alice & Wilfred Meynell	Francis Thompson DD
John Milton	Heretic in Florence CA
Alfred de Musset	George Sand CA
Sean O'Casey	Smoke ET

Coventry Patmore	Affirmative Way BA
Sylvia Plath	Schooling CA
Ezra Pound	Festal Magnet ATM
T F Powys	A Kindred Battlefield MOC/ Daybreak in Dorset MOC/ Wessex and Lyonesse BA/ Mappowder Revisited DD
John Ruskin	Friar's Crag COC/ Lake Paddle CA
St John of the Cross	Beatific Vision CA
George Sand	George Sand CA
Sappho	Leucadian Cliff ET
Shakespeare	Palazzo Rezzonico ATM
Mary & P B Shelley	Mary Shelley in Geneva ET
Jonathan Swift	Jonathan Swift: June 1723 ATM
Alfred Tennyson	Royal Wedding BA
Dylan Thomas	I Go Gentle ET
Francis Thompson	Francis Thompson DD
Virginia Woolf	Virginia Woolf Remembers St Ives DD
William Wordsworth	Lines to Wordsworth COC/ Grasmere Reflections COC/ Kirkstone Pass CA

Missionaries

Gladys Aylward	Gladys Aylward DD
Oswald Chambers	A Choice About Art DD
Jim Elliot	Jim Elliot DD
Toyohiko Kagawa	Toyohiko Kagawa BA
Henry Martyn	Henry Martyn DD
Mary Slessor	A Clash at Ikpe BA
James Hudson Taylor	Hudson Taylor to Maria ATM

Preachers

Dietrich Bonhoeffer	Dietrich Bonhoeffer DD / Jim Elliott DD
Billy Bray	After Billy Bray ET/ John Harris ATM/ Reception ATM

John Bunyan	Bunyan's Daughter COC/ Link at Oxford ATM/ Morning Call CA
John Calvin	A Calvinist in Love MOC/ Genevan Towers ET/ The Brownings at Vallombrosa ET/ Mary Shelley in Geneva ET/ Ashley Down CA/ Heretic in Florence CA
John Donne	A Night in Soho BA
George Fox	The Restored See DD
John Knox	Harpoon ET/ Testament BA/ Comeley Bank BA/ Reception ATM
Martin Luther	Katharine Luther ET/ Affirmative Way BA
John Henry Newman	Newman CA
C H Spurgeon	The Broad Winter MOC/ On the Prospect of Leaving my Birthplace ATM
[Charles Wesley	Bethel DD]
John Wesley	Testament BA/ John Wesley BA/ The Harassed Preacher BA/ The Restored See DD/ Reception ATM

Philosophers and Theologians

Peter Abelard	Affirmative Way BA
Karl Barth	The Broadening Spring MOC/ On the Death of Karl Barth ET/ Dietrich Bonhoeffer DD/ On the Prospect of Leaving my Birthplace ATM
Dietrich Bonhoeffer	Dietrich Bonhoeffer DD
[John Calvin	See under Preachers]
Hegel	Dietrich Bonhoeffer DD
Kierkegaard	Thorn in the Flesh MOC
C S Lewis	Porth Beach (Ack.) BA/ Link at Oxford ATM/ The Kilns ATM
J H Newman	Newman CA
Nietzsche	Seer and Warrier BA
Pascal	Pascal ATM
Simone Weil	Simone Weil ET

Social Reformers

Josephine Butler	Josephine Butler BA
George Muller	George Muller CA/ Ashley Down CA
Mother Teresa	Eilidh Boadella DD

Visionaries and Religious

William Blake	William Blake Notes a Demonstration ET
Jean-Pierre de Caussade	Jean-Pierre de Caussade ATM
Juan Diego	Juan Diego DD
J H Newman	Newman CA
St Bernadette	Beyond Lourdes MOC/ The Riven Niche COC/ The Frosted Image BA/ On the Prospect of Leaving my Birthplace ATM
St Francis	Reception ATM
St Margaret of Cortona	St Margaret of Cortona ATM
St John of the Cross	Beatific Vision CA
St Teresa of Avila	Mould of Castile ET
St Therese of Lisieux	Carmel COC

Artists

William Blake	William Blake Notes a Demonstration ET
Oswald Chambers	A Choice About Art DD
William Hogarth	The Veiled Sitter MOC
Holman Hunt	Holman Hunt DD
Fra Filippo Lippi	Festal Magnet ATM
Michelangelo	Fitting In CA/ Heretic in Florence CA
J E Millais	Holman Hunt DD
Picasso	The Veiled Sitter MOC
D G Rossetti	Holman Hunt DD
John Ruskin	Friar's Crag COC/ Lake Paddle CA
Andrea del Sarto	Festal Magnet ATM/ Heretic in Florence CA

| Vincent Van Gogh | The Veiled Sitter MOC/ A Choice About Art DD |
| Alfred Wallis | Porthmeor Cemetery ET/ Alfred Wallis ET |

Musicians

J S Bach	Bethel DD
Beethoven	Beethoven ET
Handel	Bethel DD
Mozart	Salieri CA
Salieri	Salieri CA
Charles Wesley	Bethel DD

Industrial and Scientific
(including Medicine and Gardening)

Alexis Carrel	St Gildas BA
William Cookworthy	Cookworthy at Carloggas ET
John Harris	John Harris ATM
Marconi	Voyages CA
Margaret Shirley	In a Truro Garden DD
'Titanic'	Voyages CA

Statecraft

Charles I	Isle of Slingers DD
Oliver Cromwell	Isle of Slingers DD
George III	Weymouth DD
Mikhail Gorbachev	Morning Call CA
Field Marshal Haig	Voyages CA
'Hiroshima'	Cloud Over Bugle CA
Lenin	Morning Call CA

Letters

Extracts from letters written by Jack Clemo to the author which throw light on JC's work:

5th April 1989:

'... I've been a Dorset townsman for nearly five years now and feel a long way from the grim Cornish clay-pit symbols of my early poetry. ... I can see why my work appeals to you, as there is the same emphasis on strength and stress in your own spiritual testimony – a rugged Nonconformity rather than the complacent jog-trot of Betjeman's Anglicanism. The Pentecostal "rushing mighty wind" seems most apparent in Nonconformist and Roman Catholic poets. Some critics detect the influence of Hopkins and Francis Thompson in my work – though I am much wider in range and have written vigorous Salvation Army poems like "Alfred Wallis", and American hot-gospel jazz pieces such as "Lunar Pentecost." I was very grateful when Bloodaxe issued my *Selected Poems* last year, and also when Lion Publishing produced Sally Magnusson's biography of me and my wife, *Clemo: A Love Story*, which sketches my spiritual history from my Methodist childhood to my present Baptist allegiance. I was a non-churchgoer for thirty years, but an isolationist poet can't write balanced Christian verse: he lacks the discipline of fellowship and his private kinks will be too obvious. ...

17th July 1989:

'...Ruth enjoys a chat with literary visitors, even though I can't join in the discussion, and the similar church backgrounds in our case will make the meeting really congenial. We can understand your sense of aesthetic and cultural isolation among average Nonconformists, as we experienced so much of it ourselves. In Cornwall I sat in my pew among villagers who said to Ruth: "Tell Jack to write something we can understand." There are exceptions in the big towns and cities where Free

45

Church people have been stirred by Francis Schaeffer's "L'Abri" movement or the Arts Centre Group which tries to vitalize the arts, even the *avant garde*, with the Christian Gospel. Schaeffer was more Fundamentalist than the A.C.G., but there was a novelty in combining broad aesthetic tastes with Biblical literalism. I'm not Fundamentalist in a sectarian or nagging bigoted sense, though I stand firm for fundamental doctrines and have used poetry and fiction to blast the limp, easy-going humanism which tolerates every kind of heresy and perversion of Christian truth. In recent months the reviewers have been labelling me "Calvinist" again because of my "*Selected Poems*," but they should have noticed that the book contains Roman Catholic and Salvation Army poems as well. ...'

31st August 1989:

'... It was good of you to give me your "*Selected Poems*" [1977]. I wish I could read them and explore your idiom and variety of themes. Christian poets are so rare nowadays, and each has his own style and emphasis. You may be more oblique in your approach than I am. I've never been content to be vaguely religious: my early poems in particular make readers face basic Christian doctrines of original sin and redemption. I'm relieved that you agree with the main idea of "*The Invading Gospel*" – that divine grace has invaded nature and natural religion and that we are saved by the grace, never by the religious "search." I believe in being charitable to all faiths, but charity should not involve a dream of unity between people whose views of God, the human soul and the life beyond death are totally irreconcilable. The instinct of worship needs the discipline and focus of the Holy Spirit: so many non-churchgoers claim they can worship in their own way without bothering about New Testament dogmas and moral standards.

You've certainly had wide experience of church practices and secular culture, and I trust Margaret [Pearce] will continue to share your personal contributions. Feminine suggestions *can* be helpful. Ruth never attempts strictly *literary* criticism of my work, but she sometimes dislikes a word I've used and tells me to substitute one that sounds less crude or is less likely to give a wrong impression! ...'

27th March 1990:

'Now I'm 74 I have no plans for more major work: I hope to publish one more volume of poems, but a poet's themes in old age tend to repeat what he has been saying for decades and the only satisfaction lies in the certainty that the themes have permanent value and will help readers, not mislead them. I'm cheered to know that you both saw something in *"The Shadowed Bed."* I think it's my best *imaginative presentation* of Christianity as well as my strongest evocation of the Cornish clay landscape and the sort of villagers I knew before I was handicapped. This type of novel isn't popular, but I don't feel I wasted those years in writing it. ...

I [wrote] a very short account of our visit to Venice which appeared, with photographs, in the January issue of *"Christian Woman."* My small book, *"Banner Poems"*, minor descriptive verse I'd contributed to the *"Cornish Banner"* was published by the Cornish nationalist press at Gorran a week after you called on us [August 1989] – a pleasant irony in view of my strictures on Cornish nationalism in *"Confession of a Rebel."* ...'

27th June 1990:

'... We spent Whitsun in Cornwall visiting friends ... We attended two Methodist chapels, tasting the old flavour. We had stayed at a vicarage on Merseyside during Easter and joined in the Anglican services with our foster grand-daughter whose father is a clergyman. Returning to our Weymouth Baptist church we had the same feeling as you describe – a freedom from rigid denominational ties. It's good to encourage a variety of churches. I believe in regular church-going now, but I doubt if I shall ever formally join a Baptist, Methodist or any other communion. I prefer to be a free-lance, supporting the basic truths held by all orthodox Christians. I seem to write more non-religious poems during the past year or two, but this doesn't indicate any loss of faith or less concern for evangelism. ...

In a permissive humanist society the Christian view isn't welcomed in fiction. I sometimes order from the Braille library a novel by some new author I've never heard of. As often as not the book turns out to be a mess of pornography – no plot, no story or characterisation – just a string of disconnected episodes in the "*Lady Chatterley*" vein. I don't bother to wear out my finger-tip on the lavish display of four letter words! Anyway, I wish you success in trying to break through with a healthier type of fiction.

Yes, Dorset does suit me for its literary associations as well as its peaceful scenery. Apart from Hardy and Powys there are other major links. I've only recently discovered that Browning's ancestors were a Dorset family. His grandfather was born in Dorset, though he moved to London before he married and Browning himself never visited Dorset as far as I know. Then there was Henry Fielding, who spent much of his youth at East Stour and gained there some impressions which he later used in the Somerset scenes of "*Tom Jones.*" I like Fielding: compared to modern pornography he could almost be called Christian, commending virtue and showing that it was Tom Jones' repentance that opened the way to his pure virginal Sophy. ...'

10th September 1990:

'The heat wave was at its height ... [we] stopped one afternoon at Buckfast Abbey [Devon], touring the monks' sanctuary and crafts centre. A bit too austere for our taste, but I wrote a poem about it which will appear in the January Arts Centre Group magazine *The Cut.* ...

Your editing of Palgrave's letters to John Murray must have been a fascinating task. I was pleased to be in the *Golden Treasury* over 20 years ago with "Christ in the Clay-Pit," but Palgrave himself would not have included it ... he *recoiled* from poems of raw religious experience – hence his exclusion of Donne from the original *Golden Treasury*, which I never cared much for. My tastes developed away from simple "popular" books. I don't know any of the Dorset authors who have emerged since T F Powys died. Some visitors here last Christmas took me and Ruth to Fleet church because, like you, they had enjoyed [John] Meade Falkner's *Moonfleet*. I've never read the novel, but what I learnt about the flooded church and the old days of smuggling inspired a poem which is to be in the 1991 *Dorset Year Book*. Nearly all my poems in recent years have stemmed from holiday visits to various places - an odd contrast to my early phase in which I could compose poems only when stuck in a clay-pit. ...

We may have a few more paddles on the Sandsfoot beach before the winds get too cold. ...'

11th December 1990:

'... The holiday glow seems remote now that a blizzard has hit Britain ... I've been tapping icy keys for weeks, preparing Christmas mail ... I'm never so busy with my literary work. I often write nothing but letters for two months or more, then there's a brief spurt of verse and the Muse is silent again for eight or nine weeks. Some poets try to force their creative vein to flow regularly, but this reduces it to a mechanical display of technical skill, never warmed by pure art or deep feeling. I've always relied on erratic and unpredictable inspiration in producing all my books – prose ones too. I know nothing of professional slickness or diligence. ...

I'm sure I would have liked your sequel to Eliot's Becket play, but alas, unless a book is in Braille it conveys little to me. Ruth can only mark a few sentences on my hand - not enough for me to judge or enjoy the whole content ...

We were cheered by your comments on my early post-marriage poems. One such poem – "William Blake notes a Demonstration" – is likely to be broadcast on Radio 4 on Sunday, 23 December in a programme called "Hot-Foot from Heaven" – time not given on the contract. I was also encouraged a month or two ago to receive the Collins anthology "*New Christian Poetry*," edited by Alwyn Marriage. This book contains a hitherto unpublished poem "The Kilns," which I wrote after visiting C.S.Lewis' home near Oxford two years ago. The year hasn't been quite blank for me, though I've often felt it as a year of small things compared with past achievements. Being nearly 75 I must be grateful to get anything published or broadcast – there was a good programme about me on Welsh radio on my 74th birthday. ...'

49

2 April 1991:

'...I came through the winter without even a cold, but only wrote two poems. Still, one of them – about converted drug addicts being baptized in the sea – was accepted by the Arts Centre Group magazine "*The Cut*" by return of post the day after my 75th birthday, which encouraged me as a sign that my writing shows no senility as yet!

I was very interested to hear that you have joined the Browning Society. He remains the only great poet who presents my blend of mysticism, realism and optimism! I would have joined the Society if I were not handicapped, but I have to stay outside as I could neither take part in its activities nor gain any enlightenment from attending its meetings. This is true regarding all local arts groups. I don't even know where the Weymouth arts centre is situated: I *might have* read my poems there had I been a normal man.

Your talks for the National Portrait Gallery must be a pleasure and profit to all concerned and also the welcome given to your Canterbury play: it's a real achievement to provide a sequel to Eliot's famous drama. Your forthcoming Stride poems sound interesting too - warm wishes for the book. It was good of you to mention me in your "United Reform[ed]" review [in the journal *Reform*] of the Collins anthology. We haven't seen it and would be very grateful if you could send us a photo-copy for my Press-cuttings album....

We've known the same problem of over-crowded bookcases. Before leaving Cornwall I gave more than fifty books to Exeter University Research library, as there was no room for them in this Weymouth house, already crammed with Ruth's and Bella's and their father's books. ...

We plan to spend Whitsun in Cornwall ... I rarely find inspiration in these visits to Cornwall: the Cornish poems I write are usually about my childhood – stray memories that flit into my mind while Dorset air refreshes me. ...'

[10th April 1991, undated postcard]:

'Thank you very much for your prompt note and the photo-copy of your review. We are delighted with your generous comment on "The Kilns" and the quotations are well chosen. ...'

15 August 1991:

'... The Whitsun week Ruth and I spent in Cornwall had seemed fresher this year and inspired two poems. A friend took us to a Salvation Army meeting at Newquay and then on a trip to Padstow, and my memories of the port blended with the bonnets and tambourines in some verses that pleased the editor of *Symphony*.

We went to Cornwall cheered by Bloodaxe's acceptance of my new collection of poems, *Approach to Murano*. I had worried about it, as the title and theme might seem incongruous from the so-called "Cornish clay-pit hermit." Ruth bought in Venice a model gondola made of Murano glass, and this became a symbol of my spiritual journey from clay to glass! Venice dominates the book, though there are many Dorset poems and a few Cornish ones in the "approach" sections. The volume should be out within a year or so – I've received my advance payment!
...
We understand how you feel about the early death of your friend ['Lawrence' in *The Goldhawk Variations*, Stride, 1999] as we have just faced the same situation. A 45-year-old cousin of mine died of cancer in Cornwall a month ago, leaving several children motherless. Such tragedies often occur and we can only accept them with a blind trust in God's overruling love. I still remain fit and mobile, though over 30 years older than my cousin. ...'

18 January 1992:

'... the visit to Browning's tomb on the anniversary of his death must have been a moving experience. I've wanted to go there ever since my mother mused in Poets' Corner in 1947, but whenever Ruth and I have gone to London we have been on a tight literary B.B.C. schedule – some show of my TV film – and had no time to visit Westminster Abbey. ...

On 14 January the Hanborough Press at Oxford [The Previous Parrot Press at The Foundry, Church Hanborough, Oxford] published *Clay Cuts*, a limited edition of some of my old claywork poems, illustrated with numerous woodcuts by Stan Dobbin. The book was launched at Liskeard Art Centre and we had agreed to attend, staying two nights with Father Benedict Ramsden [see dedication to *Approach to Murano*], who read and expounded the poems. Our prayers for relief from illness were answered just in time, and on the 13th a friend took us down to Benedict's home near Plymouth. We enjoyed the launch and I fingered a copy of the de luxe edition of *Clay Cuts*, the pictures coloured and the volume costing £52. The ordinary edition is an arty hardback selling at £18.50p. It's an interesting venture, but I get more satisfaction in anticipating *Approach to Murano*, which is all new work written in my late sixties and early seventies. ...'

16 July 1992:

' ... We're glad to know of your ... National Portrait Gallery talks on Housman and Keats – and I can understand your feelings about those "Guardian" letters, having sent so many in my youth to papers that never printed them. But being welcomed at a girls' school would have banished the newspaper disappointment for me, though I couldn't qualify for such a welcome! Your Malvern visit must have been refreshing with its music and the beauty of the hills – which I only remember vaguely, as my sight was failing when I went there in 1952.

Ruth and I had an unusual holiday in Cornwall in May. I had carried down a parcel of old MSS for the newly started Clemo collection at Wheal Martyn clay museum near St Austell. A lady manager had come to Weymouth in February and taken away spare copies of my books, some old family Bibles and a few relics, including my father's watch and my first Braille watch. While in Cornwall we visited Portholland where some of our Goonamarris furniture had been left at Dr Pat Moyer's house when we moved to Dorset. This has now been transferred to the museum, though the final lay-out for permanent display will take time. A small exhibition and a recital of my poetry have been scheduled to take place at the museum in September. It's a pity the Bloodaxe financial crisis has held up *Approach to Murano*. The firm hope to publish it in October but can't promise.

I've written a few poems this year, including one on the 1912 "Titanic" disaster which will appear in the revived "*Christian*" magazine. Its editor, Dr Alwyn Marriage, of Guildford [i.e. Surrey] University, invited Dr Donald Davie to give a lecture on my poetry at the University on 26th October. If Ruth and I can attend we shall stay a night or two at Alwyn's house – she visited us last August. ...'

15 June 1993:

'... Our visit to Guildford ... last October went well, though it followed several nightmare weeks in hospital, where I had a prostate operation only a fortnight before Donald Davie's lecture! I had already missed the Clemo exhibition and evening of readings at Wheal Martyn museum in Cornwall in September, being hospitalized at the end of August. Ruth and I enjoyed the Guildford event. We stayed at Alwyn Marriage's home. Davie gave a fine exposition of my religious poetry and we met some interesting people, poets and artists, including Heather Spears, who made sketch portraits of me and Davie.

The main advance since then was the publication of *Approach to Murano* in March. I've only had *one review so far. Selected Poems* got over a score of reviews, but the small 60-page collections don't get much notice in the Press. Modern poets depend more on public readings of their work than on printed comments. I have three readings booked for this year. The first comes on Thursday this week at Torrington Art Centre, where Paul Hyland will read my poems for an hour after fetching us from Weymouth. On 25 September he will give readings from *Murano* at Dorchester, and a further selection at Exeter on 28 October – both events being organized for Bloodaxe by South-West Arts. We hope to attend them, for though I'm 77 I still travel. ... We may go to the north of England but nowhere near Virginia Woolf's Rodmell - I still can't stand her inhuman and hollow detachment from the warm heart of everything that matters.

Our warm greetings and best wishes as ever.'

[All letters typed; signed: 1st letter 'Jack Clemo'; 2nd letter 'Jack and Ruth Clemo'; the postcard 'Jack', and the remaining letters 'Jack and Ruth'.]

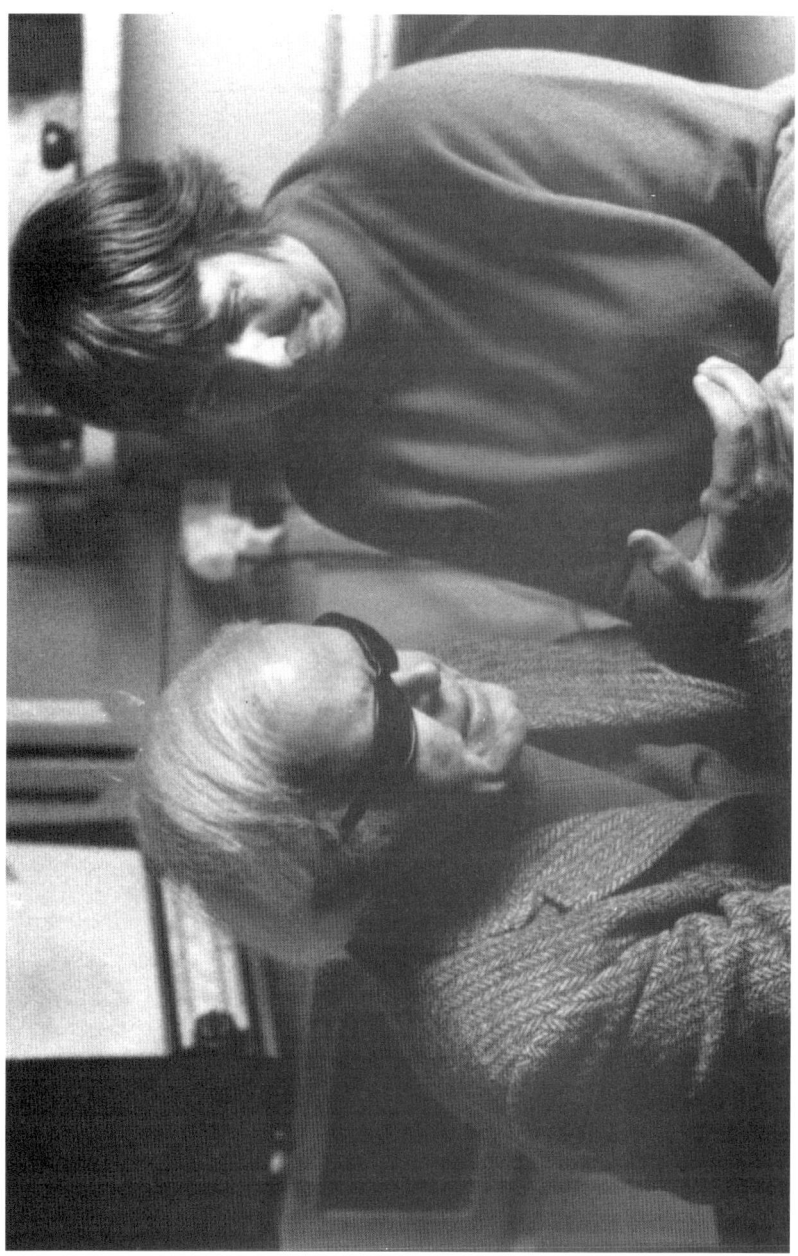

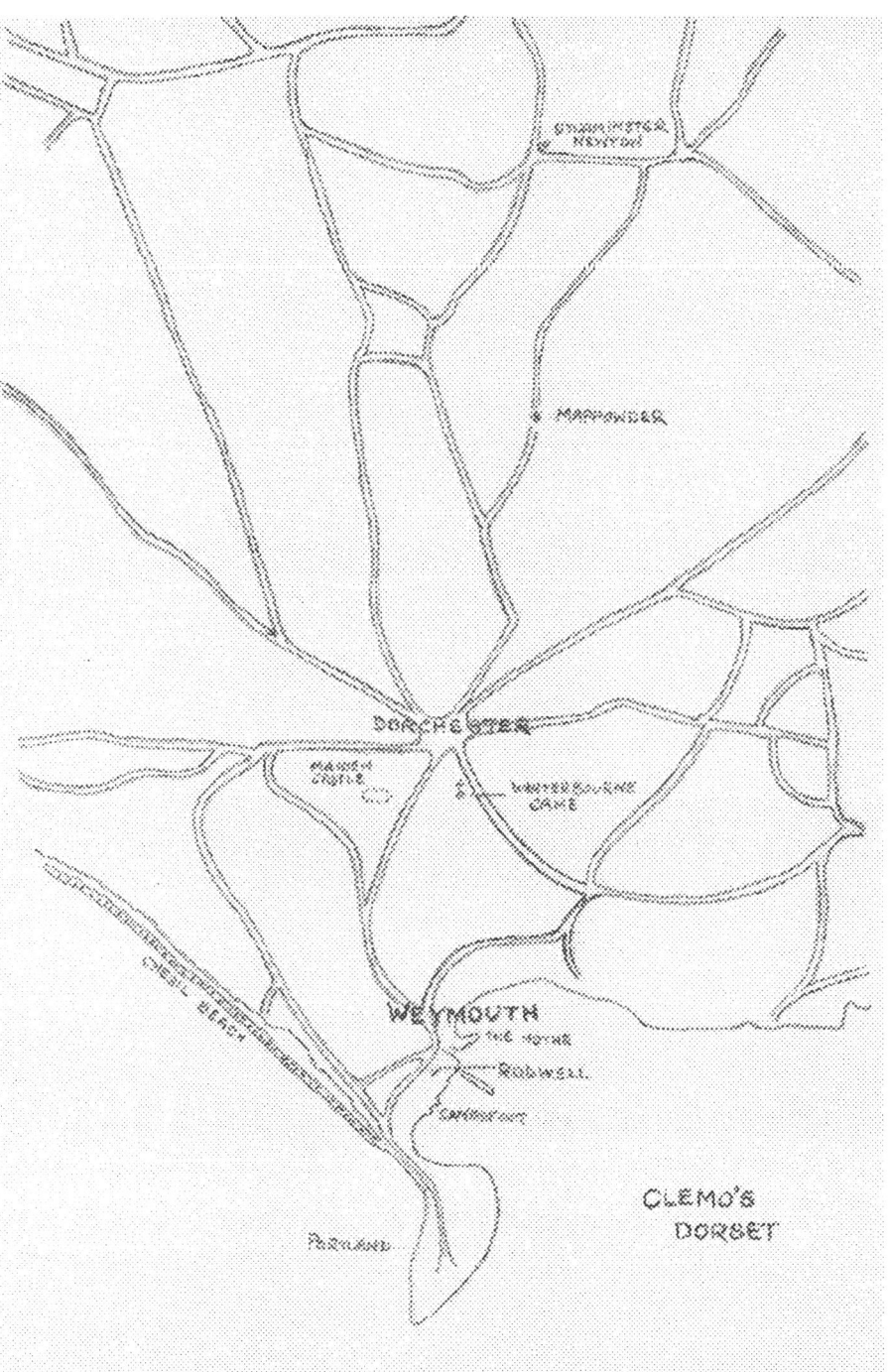

STURMINSTER NEWTON

• MAPPOWDER

DORCHESTER

MAIDEN CASTLE

WINTERBOURNE CAME

WEYMOUTH
THE NOTHE
RODWELL
SANDSFOOT

CHESIL BEACH

PORTLAND

CLEMO'S DORSET

Colloquy with Clemo

View from the Nothe

For Jack Clemo

Sheer-tongued, like the Cherbourg steamer,
leaving at night: stubborn dreamer,
you are going about all you're worth.

After loading and weighing,
unleashing your siren's lone baying,
in silence you slip from the berth

seen by the few, no one knowing
the weight of the past you are towing,
the Chesil-change since your birth

that tugs you rockways and rackward.
Past master, you go out backward,
like most men, looking to earth;

yet over-ridden by throbbing
ambition to love, be hobnobbing
with the angels caressing your thinking.

Not seeing where you are going
in the night, no other lights showing,
you keep faith with them on an inkling.

Out in the bay, you are turning
your bow to the open sea, spurning
the ignis fatuus on shore.

Small print now on the horizon,
the lights that define your hulk's prison
take on the grace we're all for.

You, the invaded, the willing
to be invaded, are filling
your lungs with the Ghost-blow you've raided.

Out past the Bill-race, you're fading
from sight amid stars now, invading
hull down, the rocked void, Gospel-maided.

1989

The Breeze at Murano

Taste, feel, smell of the sun
and the breeze at Murano,
Touch of Browning on the arm,
owning you his Muse-son.

You in verse know how to lap
at the conduit or fountain;
to paddle, dip head, and sip,
put our lips to the tap.

The caress of the breeze;
associations of Florence,
Asolo, Venice, with Robert,
provide the impulse you tease

into the passion-blown glass
of your verse, modelled on that
of the gondola Ruth
brought back from Murano. The pass

down into Italy takes you –
like all who've travelled before you
from granite and chill – through the
scent-door of the South, to a new

stratum of inspiration, one
it's never too late to quarry.
Palate of soul, you can savour
the Latin of olive and sun;

blind, toss grass like an aria,
sense it float down into thistles:
plait each blade into kisses
and crowns, in the Campagna.

Now, wherever you are.
or we are, Jack, thanks to you;
in Weymouth or London, over
Fowey or Po, in a far

city, we smell the Lagoon,
taste the moist breeze on our lips,
lap, sip and paddle, touching
the arm of one over the moon.

November 2000

Dew-of-the Sea

Here's rosemary, dew-of-the-sea. You must
have smelt it, Jack though, unlike you, it's stayed
clear of the wind, stems from the Med, shared crust

with the Romans. Often you must have played
your fingers through it, raised them to your lips
inhaling the heady herb till you had laid

up all the portent of its sensuous tips,
tasting those deeps where well-being's assured,
and fleets are ventured with no loss of ships.

All lust of mind's served by this perfume. Lured
like any lover, you bend to its breast,
bee heavy on the wind, the poem stored.

How many times your open hand has pressed
stone's rub like this, felt fossils ripple, read
pentameters to the beach and felt expressed,

reckoning vibrations with the heart and head
as earth heaved, blew, steps led, the shingle fussed
and shifted beneath you: sensed what gravel said,

the sinew's stretch, breathed registers that non-plus
the rest of us. Pebble and leaf you trust
to your inmost desk, own hand and tongue – as does

a child, an artist-scientist, a cussed
misfit of mystics, clay from birth – coo-ee
and the world shimmers in you, creature-sussed.

November 2000

63

The Sea-Monster

Even on a calm day
the great Chesil sea-monster
beats up the beach,
scoops up the sea with its great tail
and sends it bursting, breaking over
the humped and wrinkled shingle rump.

A pippa wades, scared,
retreats before it. It waves,
wants to play; to be seen as kindly,
says it won't hurt a crab.
She waves back from the years, lets it
splash spray over her, lift her up
in its arms, toss itself
at her feet; then flings
its boisterous guffawing back knowing
it dangerous.

At Sandsfoot, the unpredictable creature
greets Homer-Clemo with a wink. With a
pat on the shoulder
endears itself to him, paddles
beside him in its own shallows,
flicks him gently with its tail,
so that a few drops moisten
the poem taking shape inside his head,
as though butter wouldn't melt in its maw.

March 2002

Drink

What's in over Weymouth sands
just now? What's up in the Fleet,
reflecting sky, ruffling through
pebbles, grunting, down under
the tow, restoring, under-
cutting, sending us up, dragg-
ing us down the soon dark beach
with all we've known, on the tide?

In this bare place, there's no room
for false speech. Bowed to the wind,
head searching the light, any
trimmed wick would be welcome. It's
still to be found, round the next
bluff, above the next cove. Under the swish of this wave our
faith in our fathers is hid.

Like coke we drink, the sea seethes
as it runs through craggy teeth,
to be stomached, become por-
tion of us. The dark brown flood
as it pours over the mo-
lars hisses as it encount-
ers primeval wisdom. Un-
like coke, won't kiss and give up.

1989

The Skull, that Cockpit

Alone there, inside your skull,
you are your own mind, purely.
Sight, hearing, gone, its gull
conceives its own space, free-fally
braves it the more it is squally.

Desk-trapped, the head of water
faucets Creation, pares
the first thought, gives no quarter
to pity, turns passion's prayers
into glazed, polished wares,

treadling the wheel of inner
experience, the biff bang
thump of the blood as sinner
and saint contend in you, slang
in the head from which they sprang.

In your poems, the Word
speaks, not to be missed. 'It's in
the Book', you say when at Rodwell we meet, knit fists. The syn-
tax of faith opens win-

dows, vestals the worst, for
those who have verse and tone
of you by heart. You are more
present today than in bone,
the glory in clay of you known,

though you're alone in your
skull, that cockpit of stresses
which bank the flood at your core,
the working chest that expresses
best the thought it compresses.

November 2000

Not to Be

Not to be, that's
bad, but not to
be able to
converse or share
a new idea
because you've gone
not to bed but
ahead, that's bad,
too, though it's true
you might not have
found these pieces
tough and honest
enough. They don't
face up to the
pit and tip dai-
ly as you did
or explore the
dark side of mind
and heart like some-
one lost in mine
or Tube who tries
against the odds
of gravity

and worse to climb
up to the world
outside: to get
out and to crawl
up to the light,
even if all
one's left with when
one arrives (if
one arrives) is
a pair of dark
glasses. Is it
pitch black with no
streak of light? No,
there's always the
streak of light to
be found there, as
you told me, my
Cornish Bunyan,
coming from high
up in the top
right-hand corner.
Once seen, you could
count on it, go
for it, go up
toward it, when
no one else could
or, if they did,
never said. There
you go, that's you
all over, save
that you stuck it
out here, Jack, and
once heard won't go
away. Fact is
that, what with the
blur in my own

eye, I never
asked you the things
I meant to or
wish now I had.
It's not too late
if, where you're off
to, we'll meet. Yet
I can't count on
it as you did.
Look, I'll keep that
streak of light of
yours in my eye.

November 2000

Clay of the Ghost

Goodness, is there a way
back for you, Jack o' the West?
You are committed to
holding the Divine hand
like that of a lass
on the edge of a crevasse.

Rocked Nature shifts. Love firms
in your favour, but if
it slid you'd still stay true
to the light in your head,
implacable against giving
in to misgiving.

Self-pity is not your thing.
You oppose pessimism, what-
ever its rationale, keep
your beret on, let the tongues'
answer to Babel out-
wit the clay's devils, thwart doubt.

Crouched by this stack, close-pressed,
my clay, like yours, reads clay,
indexes graced flesh, and says
hello to its two sides:
slurry's back-sliding evangel
stayed by a good angel.

Presses close on your breath,
spring to release you. Words
of yours root. Your books seed.
You leap the crevasse as if
it was never an issue,
clay of the ghost, yet we miss you.

March 2001

At Rodwell
To Ruth and Jack

The welcoming home, the steps,
firm handclasps, tea, talk, walk
toward Portland; book and type-
writer, Jack at his desk,
locus of creation
    The wind blows from the west

Aider and abettor
of the imagination,
midwife to artefact,
your prayed life given to
him and, through him, the world
    The wind blows tongues of zest

He felt your impulse in him,
mirroring his in you,
flood insight with sight, hearing,
embodied in his letters
and poem after poem
    The wind blows where prayer wills

In Goonamarris, you'd
blight, buffet, turbulence
of circumstance, that drew
on all that love and patience
which alters environments
    The wind informs the clay

He went on climbing the
peaks of clay to glory,
you crouching by him there
writing upon his palm and
feeling his vision's touch
    The wind bodies the Word

Vowed not to cease from this,
his daily service, you
tread here and now the Fleet
fantastic, vault the drink
with him, come kingdom come
    The wind shakes roofs, shakes down

January 2001

The Powder and the Spark
For Jack Clemo and T F Powys

Tucked down amongst tree and mound,
St Peter and Paul stand rebuking
the cloverless dark. Nettled stone
and wort knit the sojourning
archangel and rogue in duetting
tryst, foil dust's predatory hound.

The hermit Powys took root here, found
the unvisited place, the spooking
quiet, the being left alone,
the thing he wanted, learning
to be one with earth, forgetting
heart's wine, in heat for the mound.

He stayed if God wasn't around.
He sat here when God wasn't looking;
when his entourage had gone
off to lunch or were earning
an honest penny, out-sweating
Adam on Mappowder ground.

Jack came, to leave profound-
ly affected, but found this booking
of grave space, talk on the bone,
not to his taste, discerning
grace in the dark, the fretting
only penitent's prayer's sound.

He sat here and found God abound-
ing, the bubbling idea cooking –
creative, redeeming – born
out of leazed pax: saw the burning
but unconsumed window, setting
match to soul-powder, clay-bound.

December 2000

Winterborne Came

Heard the cuckoo; felt pats crack
beneath my foot in the lane
from Herringston, sun on
head warm mood, as I crossed
the bourne, saw house, church, track
silver meadow and tree.

Cows in the field close packed
the fence as I passed, pulled rank
to keep pace with me, as
if to ogle and odour
me, as I took the track
that led to the Rectory.

Barnes passed along this track
to conduct evening prayer
up there amid trees. He came
to give and to receive
peace and confess soul's lack,
say grace for earth's potency.

His poetry, like Jack
Clemo's, was born of ad-
versity and words he
read in heart's book. Jack came
to lay a tribute sack
of words on the tomb-cross, be

where Barnes' earthed learning clacked
with gossip of breeze, shire tongue
of parishioners who thronged
to his funeral with
Egdon's and Lizbie's hack,
his friend Thomas Hardy.

Others came in a pack
to honour him, where he
mused twixt Whitcomb and Came,
for those of his Maiden pith,
with or without a plaque,
never lose their esprit.

Foot-and-mouth signs kept back
my steps from church and tomb
and, mazed by the main road,
I missed the Rectory.
Was I, through the senses' lack,
to lose all the poetry,

think 'unless I touch the crack
in tomb or Rectory,
I cannot come to terms
with the idea of him,
though belief, be it hear-quack,
is deadly real to me'?

I took the lane that led back
to his statue in Dorchester.
sad, until the Museum
showed me his chair and played
'Lydlinch' and 'Linden' tracks,
as I sat on shamelessly.

May 2001

Clemo at Came

I felt the Gospel flame
tongue the cross at Barnes' head,
stun me with heat, as I came
to Came at noon, my head
ready to burst with the leaven
and harnessed fervour of Barnes'
harvest faith, as we stood
by him in this quiet place.

The Son at his zenith struck
like the sun our dithering,
dallying selves, melting
the natural man, and lifting
us up in his burdened arms
here at Came, where we came
to honour Barnes' God and Barnes.

I rubbed my hands on the rough
stone of the porch and hewn cross
in the yard. I felt the Son move
on the cross in his love
and send cawing breeze, tonguing
through heart and trees: 'Christ's son,
welcome to Came, from those
here before you', as all
the daughters of Dorset.
heaven-bound from their tumuli,
leapt Conygar hill to applaud.

May 2001

Southlands Ferry
For Ruth and Jack Clemo

In Southlands Road, the ferries
to heaven pitch up and down
and through the house where Jack wrote
the Channel foams and calms
    though Jack himself's away.

From the Nothe fort the ferry
sails with its vans to France.
Down these housed slopes the holy
breezes launch heaven's ships
    from the quick quay of clay.

The creature that was forming
in warm Jurassic seas
impresses still the limestone
of the steps up to the Nothe
    though like Jack it's away.

Where once an inspiration
inhabits flesh and blood
the rock's scoured with the reckoning
the cliff's scoured by the waves
    jollied by tides at play.

The saints that stow his metre
from Westminster to Wheal
accept him, rhyme and all;
tap in the tide still on
    his hand though he's away.

The house that roofed his passion
is like another, save
that genius raised the ocean,
heard seas swell in brain's shell,
    saw rock firm from drowned clay.

    May 2002

Chesil Skip

I'm from the clay, the featureless clay sea,
night after night, the earth's dangerous belly,
heaving without direction. From my father's
white clay I came, via the red rock of Devon,
to the limestone and the marble, the Chesil stretch
of mature faith's patterning, my pebbles'
creation ordered not by size but age
and the place I'd reached in coming to myself
when I arranged them there, the swept bank whistling
and widening according to my plan.
From Browning it was a short step
over the edge of the clay-pit
to a paddle off Sandsfoot, a short
swim across the Fleet, a short
submergence of a baptism in the flood,
to emerge, my eyes adapted
to the higher shining on the celestial tips,
the angels gathering on the dazzling summits
saluting my Calvinist if buxom art
that asks kenosis of the summer hedges.
My clay hand's shaken by those ghostly shiners
my shadowy senses had the faith to greet,
seeing love move the Bill, the Chesil skip.

July 2001

Thoughts on Being a Nonconformist Aesthete[1]

I am a poet and fiction writer who was brought up as a Baptist. I am now a URC Elder and lay preacher. What follows are a few thoughts on the question of Nonconformist aesthetics (that doubtful entity) debated by Donald Davie and Daniel Jenkins.[2] The very terms of my title may strike the ear as contradictory, which perhaps says it all. Yet there are and have been such persons as Nonconformist Aesthetes – and trends, feelings, problems which I should like to bring out. I am doubtful if 'simplicity, sobriety, measure' are as significant an element in our literature as Donald Davie has suggested.[3] Hymnwriting calls for concision and a degree of simplicity, certainly. It might almost be said to be historical Nonconformity's principle mode of expression, and in the hands of someone like Isaac Watts is a self-denying genre without question. 'Mark Rutherford', the novelist, too, offer an example of sobriety but one that the case of Bunyan contradicts. There must be order, true, but a passion needing order, in what we might call our model case. There must be an emotionally charged centre; some chaos or turbulence of feeling, out of which order and meaning can be shaped by the creative artisan. There *is* often that intense feeling, I think, in Nonconformist writers, natural given the potent but unresolved prohibitions and frustrations of their situation, taken in conjunction with salvation theology, as Bunyan would have understood it. And the pressures of the latter will not be less in the psyche of the writer who is 'doubtful' or 'liberal' and who may wish to create an 'art for art's sake.' Such a writer is bound to experience *some* tension and isolation, often unguessed at by those who know him, and is likely to find himself inhabiting a no-man's land between polarised positions, be they dogmatic or liberal, religious or secular. Even Clemo, the Cornish Calvinist, more single-mindedly evangelical and clear-thinking than most, found it difficult to avoid being stereotyped and felt that his ability to empathise with Catholic and Salvationist alike was not adequately acknowledged. To the non-churchman the 'Nonconformist Aesthete' is a self-sidelined crank, an anachronistic member of a minority movement. Editors and publishers may discount his potential. Even Biblical allusions may prove more of a barrier than we realise. Amongst his co-religionists the aesthete may be distrusted as much for his aestheticism as for any doctrinal individualism or his perceived 'unreliability', an ironic form of 'Nonconformity' as it happens. That isolation has contributed to a potent individualism. It has been our writers' burden and, potentially, their glory. The more a cause of concern it is, therefore, that the literary world, in its current pre-occupation with the Booker prize winner or academically-orientated book, has denied readers the width and force of creative work on offer by this tendency to ignore original work that is not 'main stream'. Clearly this is a restrictive process that affects all minority, sectional or regional writers, and which works against independent vision and individual creativity, per se. But it is a challenge that the Nonconformist aesthete must face up to if he or she is not to succumb (a) to silence or to be unpublished; (b) to write meekly to formulae dictated by the literary establishment; or (c) to write edifying paperbacks (worthy in every sense but that of creative achievement) on the Christian Martyrs, the Christian Home, the Christian and Family Life (commonly nowadays with less prudish titles) or on How to Pray in Forty Easy Lessons. As for the writer's imaginative centre, it will have dried up.

It is true that we have an easier lot than our forebears. We don't face martyrdom, though the case of Rushdie raises anxieties there. But that brings up a point that Daniel Jenkins has touched on.[4] We are not our forebears in more senses than one. Do we have the strength of belief or feeling, still; the turmoil within; that *contrapposto*, or harmony in discord, founded on a barely harnessed agitation, essential if any significant creative consummation is to take place? There is not much doctrinal angst around, except in those fundamentalist circles where the aesthetic agony, like the open mind, is least likely to receive sympathy. Why can't moderates, doctrinal *liberals*, be passionate, too? It is true that in Clemo we have an aesthete with both angst and evangelical conviction. Yet there have not been too many other creative writers who have persisted in the Nonconformity and the angst *and* produced a significant *oeuvre*. Browning did not persist ostensibly as a Nonconformist, yet I would regard him as an exception. *His* individualism, issuing in masterworks showing the breadth of insight of a most generous spirit, arose out of passion of heart *and* intellect *and* of his Dissenting origins, surely, for it was that which had created his mental nature and – being debated, with increased tensions, within him – goes far to explain much of his subject matter as well as his feeling. Hale White ('Mark Rutherford') was thrown out of college for his doctrinal open-mindedness, and Davie himself acknowledges that he has moved away from his Dissenting (in his case, Baptist) roots.[5] D H Lawrence repudiated his Congregational origins. So the present shortage of 'passionate aesthetes' remaining Nonconformist *and* serious writers is not new. In the past they have faced important educational, financial and social barriers, though these are not so visible today.

An 'Oxbridge' education was a crucial, if not essential, entry gate both to culture and recognition at the requisite levels of publication and critical debate. Nonconformists were denied 'Oxbridge' by edict, and economic factors, too, in many cases and, until Durham and (especially) London opened early in the nineteenth century, apart from the Dissenting Academies, there was nowhere else to go. Expectation and motivation, too, will have been discouraged, given these factors and the social strata from which many dissenters (if by no means all) were drawn. This educational disenfranchisement led not only to society's literary and cultural impoverishment. It circumscribed the cultural 'reach' of an individual and severely restricted his or her contacts and standing. There could be independence and freshness of vision or, indeed, a certain energy, to be derived from confronting difficulties, but there were also potential limits to ambition or perspective and restrictions to personal growth. Much of the background, experience and stimulus contributory to sustained achievement will have been missed, and missed at *the formative moment* when it is most vital. When combined with socio-economic factors this loss could be crucial. The only alternative was to be self-motivated, self-taught, and to emerge, if at all, as a late developer. For the aspiring Nonconformist *woman*, whose claims to higher education as to suffrage were denied so much longer, this was especially applicable. Private reading, teaching and childcare, domestic or social work (including mission work) and the honing of languages or artistic skills (if there was enough money and leisure) were almost the only options. This has its effect upon a career. If you only develop in your forties or fifties it doesn't leave you too many years when your drive and capacity are at their height. Much early vision will have been lost –

including perhaps your most deeply felt and original concepts. Your *oeuvre* will inevitably be smaller than it need have been and, as for publication and recognition, you may have missed the point of entry.

It is worth spelling out what this could mean. Our self-driven, late developing writer may have had to spend thirty to forty years earning a living by some non-literary means. It may have been late on before any measure of financial independence was gained, given the unlikelihood of our Nonconformist having a private income. Writing serves and needs independence, and not only politically. Writing needs privacy, freedom from interruption; leisure to follow an idea through when first conceived – the opportunity to work at it whilst it is 'white hot'. The writer needs a room, a desk, a modicum of toast and heating, and these things cost money. The State *may* provide them – and keep the author's family from starving – but it was not always so, and the circumstances and merits of it doing so remain in question. There is little doubt but that many generations of Nonconformist would-be writers were disadvantaged here. Income will have been low; debt abhorrent, and the receipt of unearned benefit (alias 'charity') liable to induce shame in the very people most deserving of it. Earlier generations will have been denied travel opportunities, too, though not every writer needs these. Want and anxiety may break or deny a sensitive spirit, however, and there is the inability to buy books[6] or other tools or (on starting out) to subsidise publication.

Cult or sectarian values tended to limit social ambition and cultural horizons, historically. Not only did they contribute to isolation but to that excessive, group-inculcated stress on modesty, humility, guilt and self-doubt, traditionally thought of as cult-virtues. Nonconformity has understandably fulminated against hubris and assertiveness, but it has told against achievement and recognition. Many will not have *wished* to rise socially or to expend their creative strength on dinner-parties, but there can well have been a restriction of vision and a curtailment of access to social environments other than the writer's own. The restricted social mobility of the past undoubtedly hindered both worldly success and imaginative fruition. It is true that the compression of energy can increase its desire to expand and that immense force can be present in small compass, yet creative agoraphobia can result from living in an enclosed world.

Marriage was likely to be within the circle. Even the slightest variation from one's own sect (say Baptist or Brethren) was liable to be considered an unequal yoking. This, too, *could* be restrictive, socially and imaginatively, whilst any spouse (but especially a traditional Nonconformist one) *might* be unsympathetic to the aesthetic lifestyle and aspirations. I am thinking here not so much of the frugal living as the church not being the only claimant upon commitment; the books on the floor, and the 'artist' being in his 'study' for a good deal of his available time. The Nonconformity of our forebears and, to an extent, that which I experienced in (say) the 1950s, lacked a tradition of aesthetic aims or lifestyle and placed its emphasis on the commandment 'you shall have no other gods besides me.' Yet I have been wonderfully enriched by the fellow spirit who is my own partner[7], and the same has been true, I judge, for Jack Clemo. There may be delay in finding a partner, because of the confined circles (or smaller, ageing congregations), but this, with all its frustrations, may have its pros as well as its cons for a writer.

The main problems (conscious or not) will have been psychological: intensity of feeling lacking due outlet, frustration, obsession, guilt, and doubt – both in the faith and vocational sense – and the *a priori* requirement to save our own souls, which we might dispute. The great question is this:

Is art (not propaganda or apology) an acceptable goal or occupation for the Christian?

All sorts of pressures present themselves, all manner of compromises, as we each answer this question. It is a problem Catholics have wrestled with, and I was early consoled by Antonia White's comments.[8] 'Guilt' can concern subject matter, treatment or viewpoint. Ambition itself may be suspect, and many have been too modest in their aspirations. But above all: 'Is ART work?' As Bunting (Quaker in origin) makes the chairman of a conscientious objection panel say: 'Poetry ... it's not work. You don't sweat. Nobody pays for it.'[9] Personally, I believe in the triumph and value of the imagination. Some of my books issue from that belief.[10] But it is a confidence that is still shaky and hard-won, in my mid-fifties. No wonder so many opt out. For how *does* one justify it (and find the necessary time for it) in the face of the meetings and pastoral concerns, the preaching and family life, the autumn socials and the New Year parties, daily employment and other interests or needs - especially that, so often unexpressed and unmet amongst Nonconformists, of emotional satisfaction and relaxation? One has to choose, and to plump for the aesthetic is still to risk being misunderstood. One might brave that, but one has to convince *oneself*. Our aesthetic aspirations can seem disturbingly egoistic, unorthodox and tangential to the Free Church community's main concerns, yet, the 'non-church' world may seem even more alien. Tension and 'guilt' can be the result.

In the traditional chapel context, an 'ivory tower' approach can be especially suspect. Fellow worshippers will ask that the writing be intelligible and accessible; have obvious meaning, and be edifying, and who can blame them? It is something that Jack Clemo came up against, as well as the writer.[11] It musn't be too 'clever' or involve Joycean word-play or appear to enjoy itself for its own sake. Experimental or 'play' aspects are unlikely to be appreciated. Yet Nonconformist writing must exceed its grasp, surely; be willing to take risks, and be vulnerable. It should aim high; not play safe or be tame. It should have emotion to harness and exercise over it a tight control. It should not eschew paradox or surprise – and would that such qualities were in more of our sermons! Likely elements will be the Confessional; the Testimony[12]; the Personal – especially the development of the writer's inner life, its 'spiritual' progress or regress, the movements of a 'soul' – together wih related autobiographical preoccupations. In this it is not unconnected with the Romantic concern with self-fulfilment. There may be repressed drives which may work adversely or lead to strong and sympathetic writing. There may be elements cribbed or obsessive in tendency, accompanied by limitations of subject range or setting. There may be visionary elements of extreme force and originality, born of the Nonconformist imaginative ethos – possibly having root in the Bible and/or, as in Clemo's case, of doctrine. The tug of upbringing may bring prohibitions and create tensions yet lead to unique creativity that vibrates through the years. The Jewish Kafka's profound, if sombre, achievement *The Trial* is exactly the kind of writing that we might expect from the sort of sectarian ghetto that Nonconformity certainly *was*. *Pilgrim's Progress*, triumphantly, springs from – and is indivisible from – its own doctrinal and Biblical roots.[13, 14] The lack of ease or security; the tensions produced by 'guilt' or 'fear', as well as sheer aspiration, have all contributed, as the clash of 'cultures' has gone on in the writer's mind. Can we keep our feet in the sacred circle, yet walk in the world? Can we put art 'first' yet stay loyal to our Lord? By God's grace one may do it. But the temptation remains: to jot the poem in secret, in the back pew, and to keep the Bible out of sight in one's work as well as when out in 'the world'. Yet if, for our earnest aesthete, the worst thing is to aim low, the saddest is to give up.

Notes

1   The paper published in *Reformed Quarterly*, Vol.3, No.3, Oct/Nov 1992, 6-8, with revisions and additions.

2   Donald Davie *A Gathered Church*, Routledge, London, 1978; Donald Davie *Dissentient Voice*, University of Notre Dame, Indiana, 1982; Donald Davie, 'Nonconformist Poetics', *Jrnl. URC Hist. Soc.*, Vol.3, No.9 Oct 1986, pp.376-385; Daniel Jenkins, 'A Protestant Aesthetic?', *Ibid.*, pp.368-376

3   Davie, *A Gathered Church*, p.25; Jenkins, *art.cit.*,pp.368 ff.

4   Jenkins, *Ibid.*, pp. 372-6

5   Davie, *A Gathered Church*, p.1

6   Where would we be without public libraries!

7   Margaret (nee Wood), my *wife*, in case of misunderstanding.

8   Antonia White, 'The Novelist', in J M Todd, ed., *The Arts, Artists, and Thinkers*, Longman, 1958, pp.110-120

9   Basil Bunting, *Collected Poems*, 2nd ed., Fulcrum, 1970, pp. 130-131 ('What the Chairman told Tom')

10 [Brian Louis Pearce] *Victoria Hammersmith*, 2nd ed., 2001, *Tribal Customs*, 1997, *The Goldhawk Variations*, 1999, and the story 'Syon' celebrate the triumph of the imagination. *Jack o'Lent*, 1991 (poetry), is charged with the impact of Easter. *London Clay*, 1991, treasures the sunlight and the forgiveness of sin. *The Tufnell Triptych*, 1997, wryly

considers aspects of English religious experience. 'Syon' has echoes of Bunyan and, like 'Mrs Wilder's Guest', Biblical parallels. Other relevant titles include *Shrine Rites*, 1990, *The Damien Offices*, 2000, and *The Widow of Gozo*, 2002 (plays); the '*City Whiskers*' sequence 1996 (poetry) *Battersea Pete* 1994 (fiction), and the forthcoming *St Zacchs* (fiction) in which the dynamic of personal response is shown as unifying diversity. See Note *13*.

11   'Tell Jack to write something we can understand' (letter of Jack Clemo to BLP, 17th July 1989) – and Jack was a clear minded writer who did not go in for word-play.

12   Cf. several papers read to the Birkbeck College *Religion and Society* History Workshop held at Friends' House, London, 7-9, July, 1983.

13   Not least those time-honoured Dissenting principles: the Gathered Church (the company of believers and seekers in a particular fellowship); the Priesthood of all Believers; the Supremacy of Scripture as guide to doctrine and action, as interpreted through the Holy Spirit (a tenet which may be as valid for a devotional liberal as for a fundamentalist), and Personal Response to God-with-us-in-Jesus or, more traditionally, what God has done in Jesus.

14   Andrew Duncan in his 'Protestantism as a component of regional culture' (published on his website), a rich text which cites George Fox, Lucy Hutchinson, Baxter, Bunting, the Covenanters, the Catholics Patmore and Barker, *and much else*, does not mention 'Mark Rutherford' or Clemo, but neither does it treat of Bunyan, oddly, perhaps.